what color is
Monday?

what color is
Monday?

How Autism
Changed One Family
for the Better

CARRIE CARIELLO

Publisher's Cataloging-in-Publication

Cariello, Carrie.
　　What color is Monday? : how autism changed one family for the better / Carrie Cariello.
　　p. cm.
　　LCCN 2012953910
　　ISBN 978-0-9847927-3-3

　　1. Cariello, Carrie—Family. 2. Autistic children—Biography. 3. Parents of autistic children—Biography. 4. Families. 5. Autistic children—Family relationships.　I. Title.

RJ506.A9C37 2012　　　　　　618.92'85882'00922
　　　　　　　　　　　　　　QBI12-600222

Portions of this book have previously appeared (in slightly different form) in *Autism Spectrum News*. Some of the names in this memoir have been changed.

Riddle Brook Publishing LLC, Bedford NH
www.riddlebrookpublishing.com
www.whatcolorismonday.com

For my family

Thank you for bringing so much color to my life.

Contents

NOTE TO SELF   1

EARLY DAYS   7

JACK   15

BEWARE THE BUSY UROLOGIST   23

SNOWFLAKES   31

MAKING PROGRESS: STRETCH, DON'T BREAK   43

MY PAPER BOY   55

WHEN WE CAN'T FIND THE WORDS   61

COOKIES FOR DAD   69

A LETTER TO HENRY   77

LESSONS AT THE YMCA   81

THE PEOPLE WE MEET   91

DOGS ON PARADE   97

A LETTER TO JOEY   107

WHAT DOES HEAVEN LOOK LIKE?   113

OBSESSION   123

KARATE   129

A LETTER TO ROSE   135

ANXIETY AND MEDICATION   139

CARIELLO CRUISE   149

A LETTER TO CHARLIE   163

BELIEVE AND BREATHE   167

THE AUTISM IN ALL OF US   181

SIGNS   187

A LETTER *FROM* JOEY   191

WHERE WE ARE NOW   195

A LETTER TO JACK   207

Note to Self ✦

NOT LONG AGO I READ an article featuring a family and their newly diagnosed autistic son. The headline shouted something like "Housewife Fights to Save Her Son!" When I read this, I felt a surge of outrage.

Save? *Save?*

After a moment my sense of indignation subsided, and I thought to myself, "Oh, I remember those days," days of thinking we had to somehow help our son recover from his autism, to heal him and change him, to discard his diagnosis like a caterpillar escaping a cocoon, leaving us with a beautiful, bright-eyed boy who made eye contact and loved birthday parties. Now I know better.

My next thought was that I should write her a letter telling her to relax, not to worry, that it's all going to work out. Luckily, before I actually sat myself down to pen such a note,

I realized she probably wasn't too interested in what I had to say.

But I did think about what I wished someone had told me when Jack was first diagnosed, what I would have liked to have known. And so instead I decided to write a letter to myself, dated the day two-year-old Jack was diagnosed by our developmental pediatrician.

November 3, 2006

Dear Self,

Today you received Jack's official diagnosis. You expected this news all along, but you're still reeling from the doctor's softly spoken words. You listened attentively to his hushed voice saying things like *considerable delay* and *early intervention* as Jack whirled and spun around the tiny exam room. At one point you started to sweat.

It's been a long journey leading up to this day, a long road of *when will he talk* and *why doesn't he recognize me*. A long two years of tantrums, heartache, and the eerie quiet of a toddler who doesn't speak. Months of watching your brown-haired boy through a two-way mirror as a variety of specialists tested his hearing, tested his language, tested the way he stacked multicolored blocks.

Autism.

Right now, you're thinking you can fix him, that he will outgrow this. But you can't, and he won't. Instead, both you and he will learn to coexist with it, and in the process you'll discover how grateful you are to be privy to the miracle of his mind.

Slowly, steadily, you're going to see Jack for everything he is rather than what he is not. The list of *he's not talking when will he point why doesn't he play with others* will eventually be replaced with *look at his smile I love to hear his voice tell me again Jack tell me everything you have to say tell me.*

He will surprise you every single day.

In the meantime, I won't lie. You have some very long days ahead of you, days full of frustration, of intense outbursts, of whining. Days where you'll go to bed at night hating yourself because you feel you haven't done enough or haven't done it right. But you will always wake in the morning with renewed resolve and determination because deep down you know he needs your strength.

You're going to question your decision to continue working while sending him to childcare a few days a week. Don't. The time you spend away from him will fuel your time together; it is essential to have those mental and emotional breaks. Otherwise autism will consume you altogether.

In the summer of 2007 you'll spend meal times chasing him around the kitchen and planting him back in his chair, over and over and over again. You'll wonder if it's worth it. I assure you it is; by the time he's six Jack will be a pleasure at the dinner table.

At times you are going to marvel at his progress, his giant leaps in communication and social behavior. Then for a while, nothing. His development will level off, and you'll fight a rising panic that he'll never move forward again. Don't worry. Like the steps on a staircase, his pattern will be to jump up and then stand still for a while.

He will teach you to see days as colors.

CARRIE CARIELLO

Jack's going to latch onto subjects, things like cars and license plates and seemingly random dates. As you continue to open your own mind to autism, you'll start to understand what it all means to him. And so it will be meaningful to you.

You are going to meet some extraordinary people in the next few years, and your idea of a hero will change dramatically. Heroes will be the bubbly blonde preschool teacher who patiently coaxes sentences from Jack's lips and the rail-thin painter from Texas who good-naturedly lets your son play country music on his radio while the front porch gets a fresh coat. It will be a man who sits beside his dog in a hotel lobby and ever so gently persuades Jack to *come closer, closer, closer Jack we're waiting for you*, until Jack reaches out a tentative hand and breaks down a phobia with a quick stroke of soft, tan fur.

Your biggest hero will be the dark-haired man you married.

You're also worried about how Jack's autism will affect the dynamic with his siblings. Please trust me that the relationship between these children is going to blossom into something extraordinary. You are all going to change for the better because of him.

You will find new ways to channel your stress, things like running and writing and yoga. Maybe you'll even run a marathon. In learning to manage the endless demands of autism and a family, you will also learn to take care of yourself.

And although you'll start to understand that you can't save Jack, you will never, ever give up on this incredible boy. One day there will be a beautiful moment when the boy and the autism combine and you fiercely love them both.

4

He's eight now, and I can't wait for you to meet him.

Oh, and one more thing. If you think today was crazy, you might want to brace yourself. Because tomorrow you're going to find out you're pregnant.

Love,

Me

P. S. It's a girl.

Early Days ᴗ

"I CAN NEVER MARRY YOU," I told the dark-haired guy preparing dinner at the stove. "That would make me Carrie Cariello!"

It was my first date with a college student named Joe. I'd met him while I was waiting tables at Pizzeria Uno's. He was one of the cooks who stood behind the window and slid dishes of food down the long stainless steel counter for the servers to reach. The first thing I noticed about Joe was his sleek, muscular forearms. The second thing was his voice; it was smooth and gentle as he called out things like "Food's up!" and "Eighty-six broccoli soup!" This was in the summer of 1994, and we were both about to start our junior year at the State University of Albany in New York.

For our date he made me chicken stir-fry in a worn-out stainless steel frying pan. I sat at the white Formica table in the kitchen of his downtown apartment as he sautéed chicken and vegetables.

Standing with his back to me in a plaid flannel shirt and jeans, he seemed confident as he deftly flipped the food around. It was when he turned around to hand me the plate that I saw his nervous smile. I was touched to notice he'd peeled and sliced all the vegetables beforehand and had organized them into individual plastic bags.

I was also deeply touched as I listened to him talk about his family while we ate: his Italian parents, his five siblings, and his twelve nieces and nephews. I was touched to hear him earnestly explain his plans for dental school and a family of his own. Four years later I married him, and became, for better or worse, Carrie Cariello.

We still have that frying pan.

When we got married Joe was starting his second year of dental school in Buffalo, New York, and I was working in the marketing department of a small construction company. For the next three years we lived in a two-bedroom apartment that had a front porch, a pool, and an enormous Rottweiler named Deuce (who lived downstairs with the landlords). Although we had a lot of fun using the pool, we decided to start house-hunting as soon as Joe graduated. We were tired of the barking.

One Sunday, following Mass at the church in our town, we took a long walk through the tree-lined neighborhoods of a small village called Snyder and noticed a For Sale by Owner sign on a brick colonial halfway down a quiet street. Though the sign mentioned an open house later that afternoon, we barged on in and asked to see it early. It was everything we hoped for: a charming, three-bedroom home in a beautiful neighborhood. We returned to our apartment, giddy with excitement.

That night I dreamed of baby boys.

The next afternoon we sat in the breakfast nook with the sellers and presented an offer. They accepted at once. Sitting in a kitchen full of chipped white cabinets and a dangling light fixture shaped like a bird's nest, Joe and I bought our first home.

Throughout the fall we worked to make the house our own. We stripped wallpaper, painted moldings, and chose countertops. With the help of Joe's parents and friends we renovated the kitchen and painted the dining room a deep pumpkin color. One night we had friends over for dinner, and as we proudly showed off the bedrooms, the hardwood floors, and the kitchen, their young daughter told her father in a loud whisper, "I think it's time they had some kids in this house." That comment stuck with me throughout the evening.

I've sometimes been too casual with my birth control pills, and when you combine that with exhaustion and a missed period, the math isn't all that complicated. Early the next morning I did a quick calculation and then dug out an old pregnancy test I had left over from some previous scares. I shouldn't have been surprised at the results, but I was.

I was shocked. So surprised that I burst into hysterical tears. As many women can explain, there's nothing like the emotional turbulence packed into those few moments following a pregnancy test that displays two lines (or plus signs, or smiley faces). Much like motherhood itself, there's no way to prepare for (or to predict) how it's going to feel until you're sitting in your bathroom watching that ridiculously expensive stick change color.

Although we knew we'd have a family together, Joe and I hadn't yet discussed a timeline for getting pregnant. He was as surprised as I was and nearly speechless when I ran in to wake him up by waving the test in front of his half-opened eyes. (Note: it would not be the last time he'd be struck dumb when presented with the results of a pregnancy test.)

The next few weeks passed with dizzying excitement. Joe and I decided not to share the news with everyone just yet (except for my sister, Sarah, and my closest friend, Melissa). But when we were alone we talked of nothing but the baby, baby, baby. Boy or girl? Should we find out? What color should the room be?

Then one day at work I noticed a quarter-sized drop of blood when I went to the bathroom. Panicked, I called Melissa, who insisted that I head to the emergency room just to hear the heartbeat and have some assurance that everything was fine. I called Joe and had him meet me there. After an hour of waiting Joe had to return to see patients. Dr. Gross was unreachable, so a hospital technician performed the sonogram. It turned out to be a very long afternoon.

Some memories will stick with you forever; specific points in time where every detail, every nuance, is etched in your mind. I will never forget that sonogram, nor the technician's cheery hello, too quickly followed by the sudden clench of her jaw as she searched the screen. I remember her calling the radiologist over, a slight Indian man in a plum-colored shirt, and murmuring something softly to him, then asking in a louder tone if he'd like to talk to me. Most of all, I remember the slight shake of his head and the wave of his hand as he turned on his heel and walked out of the room. It was as if, with that single gesture, he'd waved the pregnancy away himself.

Joe returned to pick me up and we went home, both of us devastated.

The days following the miscarriage were incredibly trying, as I cycled through both anger and loss while my hormones raged and my body worked to return to its pre-pregnant state. It's difficult to imagine how much you can grieve the loss of something you barely had.

We tried to conceive again almost right away. There were five long months of tantrums (me), crying (me), and melt-downs (also me). Five months of bewilderment (Joe), empty assurances (Joe), and more crying (still me). I pictured us moving through life childless, generating forced gaiety over other people's children while we each massaged the holes in our hearts. Luckily, by July we were blessed with another positive pregnancy test and another bout of hysterical tears. I suppose that in the scheme of things five months really isn't a long time compared to what many couples have to endure, but it sure felt like an eternity at the time.

Despite my anxiety about another miscarriage, what followed was a blissful and joyous pregnancy. Awaiting the arrival of our firstborn was one of the happiest times in our lives, and surrounded by friends, family, and colleagues, we eagerly anticipated our new baby. On March 22, 2003, we welcomed our son, Joseph Anthony Cariello. (Or Boochie, as we curiously nicknamed him early on—and still call him to this day.)

We were thrilled, and no one was prouder of his new son and namesake than Joe, a devoted father from the very first moment. He changed all of the diapers in the hospital and held his son constantly between feedings. He was at once gentle and sure with his tiny newborn, swaddling our child and holding him close when he cried, patting his back to release bubbles of air. When it came time to roll the bassinet to the nursery so we could sleep, Joe wept.

We returned home the next day, and Joe's enthusiasm for fatherhood continued. Exhausted, I settled in for an early afternoon nap, only to wake and discover both the proud father and our new baby gone. Unable to contain his excitement and pride, Joe had buckled Joey into the infant car seat and walked over to show his new son off to the neighbors. He delighted in every finger, every toe, even every diaper.

First-time motherhood is kind of a blur to me, but I do remember it was harder than I'd expected. (And anyone who tells you it was easier than expected is lying.) Although Joey was a pretty easy newborn, I was thoroughly unprepared for the sleep deprivation and the tedious tasks that accompany caring for a baby: the diaper changes, the pacifiers, the constant feedings, the extra laundry. I started to miss my freedom and my job. As much as I loved the little guy and the extraordinary pleasure that came from nursing and snuggling with him, I also found that being at home all day with an infant could sometimes get kind of boring.

After two months Joey began a more predictable sleep schedule, and I was able to return to work four days a week. Joe also worked four days, so by staggering our schedules we each had a day to enjoy Joey on our own. We spent our weekends pushing the stroller through the neighborhood and watching him grab for his toes, all the while reassuring ourselves that of course he was the cutest baby ever. And really, he was.

Joe's parents took the long drive up from where they lived in Lake Carmel for a visit in July, and while Joe was out with them I started once again to do some rudimentary math in my head. Joey was four months old and I was still nursing, but my cycle had started about three months after he was born and I'd just recently realized that it had made a brief appearance and then disappeared again. I broke into the emergency stash of pregnancy tests and, sure enough, two lines (and hysteria) once more. At just about the same time Joe and his parents returned, and I distinctly remember holding Joey in my arms and frantically calling Joe up to the bedroom while his parents began preparing dinner.

He was ecstatic.

Jack ❧

I WAS A LITTLE OVERWHELMED at the idea of another child so quickly, but we were enjoying our first so much that I quieted my anxiety. I knew it would be great for Joey to have a sibling so close in age, and deep in my heart I hoped for another boy.

With the maternity clothes barely packed away, we announced to our surprised family and friends that I was expecting again. I enjoyed another easy, pleasant pregnancy, and John Michael made his way into the world on Mother's Day of 2004. Except for his size—nine pounds, three ounces—his delivery was fairly brief and uncomplicated. We called him Jack right away.

We brought Jack home that Monday and settled into life with our two boys; since they were a little over a year apart, we basically had two babies. Joey was still crawling when Jack was born, and I spent a lot of my time nursing Jack in a large, blue recliner while watching Joey playing on the floor and cruising the furniture.

Those of you who know Jack may be surprised to learn that he didn't spring from the womb demanding to know the obstetrician's birth date or the color of his radio. Instead, he emerged coughing, sneezing, and fussing. He developed congestion when he was about three weeks old and battled a seal-like bark and a dripping nose from that point forward. His cough literally stopped people in their tracks; women would approach me in the grocery store and ask why he sounded so sick.

Having a constantly sick baby was incredibly stressful. Joe and I worried about him nonstop and we were exhausted from walking him around the house night after night to soothe his ear pain. Several visits to an ear, nose, and throat specialist revealed reflux, along with repeated ear infections.

Eventually five-month-old Jack landed in the operating room where he had tubes inserted in his ear drums and his adenoids removed. The idea of surgery when he was so little terrified us, but both Joe and I felt we had no choice. (Note: it turns out that Jack wasn't the only child who would require tubes. Eventually all five kids had the procedure. A doctor once told us that we made cute babies with bad ears.)

We were hopeful things would now get easier, that Jack's constant fussiness would subside, but we were wrong. The medical concerns of reflux and ear infections had been addressed, but we soon faced other concerns.

I have a vivid memory of taking the two boys to our

favorite Italian restaurant in Buffalo. Joey was about a year-and-a-half old and Jack nearly six months. They were both wearing identical blue pajamas covered in a pattern of snow-flakes, and Jack was sitting up in a high chair for the first time. As we enjoyed a pleasant meal, people stopped by our table to comment on their closeness in age and how alike they seemed. All in all, a lovely evening. So why does this memory make me so sad?

Because it's the last time I remember not worrying about my son.

I can't point to any particular light-bulb moment when I knew with certainty that Jack had autism, but I always had a gnawing pit in my stomach and a strong sense that some-thing was just not right. His language wasn't developing nor-mally. He never pointed or gestured, and he had a difficult time managing solid foods. Jack rarely made eye contact, and he didn't babble or coo. He rarely seemed content in his own skin. He fussed constantly and was difficult to soothe.

His sleep pattern was irregular, and he woke often in the night, even after he turned a year. Joe and I would bring him downstairs and watch *Baby Einstein* videos with him over and over and over until he grew drowsy enough to go back to bed. I remember sitting with Joe during one of these noc-turnal movie showings and telling him, "Something's wrong with Jack. You know something is wrong."

And tantrums? He could rage and bang on the floor for what seemed like hours, and we were never sure why.

People often ask me how I knew something was amiss

with Jack and how old he was when we noticed the warning signs. Autism unfolds differently in each individual; some demonstrate symptoms very early on while others grow and interact normally for a while and then seemingly morph into another person altogether. From what I've read and heard from other parents, the development of this tricky disorder is as unique as the minds of autistic people themselves.

With Joey only a year older than Jack, it was easy for me to calculate the milestones my younger son should have been reaching. His social skills were way behind. I kept waiting and waiting for the day he would push his fat little feet into our grown-up shoes and shuffle around the kitchen to make us laugh, the way I'd seen Joey and countless other small children do. I kept waiting for him to play peek-a-boo or ask for the Itsy Bitsy Spider song by linking his fingers together.

I waited for him to recognize me, but to Jack we were more like tools than people. He would take my arm and lead me to the refrigerator or to a toy he wanted, placing my hand on the desired object. We'd play a game at mealtimes where my husband would point to me and repeat, "Mommy! Jack, look at Mommy! This is Mommy." But Jack seemed to have no idea who we were. It was chilling.

In the winter of 2004, when Jack was about eight months old, our pediatrician referred us to Early Intervention services for an evaluation, and we started to acquaint ourselves with unfamiliar terms like "joint attention" and "self-directed." Joint attention is when two (or more) people share attention or emotion about the same thing; while Joey, for example, would point out the window at a puppy walking by and try to direct my attention to the scene, Jack had no such skill. He never engaged us for anything—he preferred doing things completely by himself, like getting milk or a toy rather than trying to communicate his needs. This behavior, we were told, showed how Jack was "self-directed," an indication that he was not relating to others in a typical manner.

I sat through many, many painful sessions watching as a speech therapist tried to coax language from my son or engage him in pretend play. During those early intervention tests there was one particular game each therapist played— the fake birthday party. The counselor would drag out some grubby baby doll, the kind whose eyes flutter up and down, and construct a pretend birthday cake out of Play-Doh. He or she always started cheerily chirping about how "It's Baby's birthday! Can we sing to Baby?" while Jack sat there stiffly or, sometimes, tried to grab for the doughy cake. I watched this seemingly ridiculous scenario unfold enough times to finally ask why, why the Play-Doh cake? Why the bald little doll and the cheerful singing? It seemed like Jack's entire future was riding on this birthday party, and he didn't even know the words to the song.

One of the many counselors who conducted this test explained she was looking for pretend play, to see if Jack could follow along with an imaginary party and participate. And he couldn't.

By the time Jack was sixteen months old we had a speech therapist and a special education teacher working with him weekly, and we were still having him tested to figure out the source of his language delay. One doctor suggested a hearing test, and my spirits actually soared. Deaf! Why, maybe he was deaf! We could work with that! Even though I knew that Jack could hear someone open a bag of animal crackers from three rooms away, I fostered a tiny seed of foolish hope that maybe, just maybe, he was hearing impaired and that all of this could be solved with a simple crash course in sign language.

Nope, not deaf.

Many people were adamant that we were overreacting. We heard one explanation after another about how Jack's older brother was talking for him or how children developed at their own pace. How he was fine, just fine, and we should give it time. During this time I learned a very valuable lesson; we were Jack's family, in the final analysis his only advocates, and we needed to follow our instincts and voice our concerns. Loudly.

In the middle of November our third son, Charlie, was born. Joey was two and a half, and Jack just eighteen months old. When I brought his new brother home Jack didn't even react, striding past me as if I were a floor lamp (okay, a chubby floor lamp in stretch pants, but you get the idea). He seemed to have no attachment to me whatsoever. My sister came to visit, and for the first time someone in my family validated my fear. As she watched him trace the same grout line with his finger over and over again, she gently agreed that, yes, maybe there was something off. She commented, too, on how she'd seen him withdraw when things became chaotic, almost as though he had an inner world he preferred.

But there were also hopeful moments, instances that encouraged us. Early one afternoon, two-week-old Charlie was swaddled and dozing in his swing. I watched quietly from the couch as Jack made his way wordlessly over to him, bent down like an oversized hummingbird, and kissed him tenderly on the forehead. Then without a sound he straightened up and walked away. No mother has ever loved her child more than I loved my mysterious, wondrous little boy in that moment.

When Charlie was six weeks old I went back to work part-time, and Joey and Jack both returned to childcare. One day a photographer came to the center to take class pictures and I went in to see if I could help. Jack was about two, and I remember sweating as I chased him around the playroom, trying to get him to listen to me. The photographer—a stooped man in his sixties with thinning white hair—brightly chirped, "Don't you worry! I work with autistic children all the time!" His words stopped me cold. I cried all the way home.

Not long after the elderly man from Teddy Bear Portraits started connecting the dots, we had a long-anticipated appointment with a pediatric specialist in Buffalo. Jack and

I were cramped into his small office as the doctor administered yet another set of tests aimed at gauging Jack's level of speech and engagement.

In the middle of the testing, Jack bumped his shin on the corner of a metal filing cabinet, and he started to shriek and whirl around frantically. The doctor looked at me and asked, "Does he ever come to you for comfort when he's hurt?" That very question, that very moment, crystallized every fear I'd ever had about my beautiful brown-haired, blue-eyed son. More than his language deficiency, more than his limited eye contact, more than his horrific outbursts day after day and the fact that he didn't care if some plastic doll named Baby had a pretend birthday party or not, the cold truth was that Jack never sought comfort from me.

Time stood still.

A few minutes later the doctor gently told me what I'd been expecting to hear for some time: Jack had an Autism Spectrum Disorder (ASD), specifically, Pervasive Developmental Disorder (PDD).

The very next day we discovered I was pregnant with our fourth child.

Beware the Busy Urologist ﹀

I'VE HEARD PARENTS OF autistic children describe a period of grieving and bereavement immediately after hearing the diagnosis, a time during which they mourned the loss of a normal child. While very understandable, I never experienced sadness in that way, I think because I always knew with certainty that something was wrong, that Jack wasn't developing normally. Frankly, I was relieved to have a name for it, to be able to explain why Jack would rather spend play dates with the vacuum than with his friends. It was a relief that I wasn't crazy; something was amiss with our adorable little boy, and we needed help.

We accepted the diagnosis and forged ahead, getting Jack as many early services as we could. I do think in the back of our minds we both harbored the notion that he would outgrow this, that his symptoms would diminish and he would blossom into a typical child.

Soon after we received Jack's diagnosis in November 2006, we started thinking seriously about moving. We didn't have any family in Buffalo, and Joe was anxious to be somewhat closer to his parents while our children were young. Having been an associate for nearly five years, he was also ready to own his own practice and truly launch his career.

I, on the other hand, didn't really want to move. I loved Buffalo. Over the course of ten years we'd made a great number of friends, we lived in a beautiful little house on a tree-lined street, and I enjoyed my job. Also, we'd just enrolled Jack in an integrated preschool five days a week, and I was reluctant to uproot him. It seemed like we'd been on such a long road up to this point, and now we finally had some support in place.

For months Joe and I reviewed the pros and cons of moving our little family, frequently staying up long after the three boys were in bed and discussing whether to stay or leave. Although the thought of saying good-bye to Buffalo was painful for me, Joe wanted more than anything to be closer to his family. In addition, he'd been exploring dental practices throughout Western New York without much success; if we didn't look elsewhere his career would stall.

And so we agreed: it was time for a change. He began looking throughout the Northeast for practices to buy and before long found one in New Hampshire, not far from where

Joe's brother lived (and several hours closer to his parents). In April 2007, when I was seven months pregnant, we moved to the town of Bedford, a partly rural suburb just outside of Manchester, New Hampshire's largest city. Joey had just turned four, Jack was about to turn three, and Charlie was seventeen months.

We'd chosen Bedford largely based on the proximity to Joe's new practice, and unknowingly (and very fortunately) we'd chosen a school district well known for its special education program. In the months before we left Buffalo I'd spent a fair amount of time communicating with the director of the Bedford Early Education Program (amusingly abbreviated as "BEEP") in order to organize Jack's entry into their preschool program; he started just a week after we moved.

I remember leading Jack down the hushed hallway of Memorial School accompanied by his new teacher, Emily. He was still in diapers, and his chubby legs made a soft rustling sound against the fabric of his blue jeans. As we rounded a corner and Jack reached up to hold her hand, she broke into a radiant smile and said, "He's already further ahead than I expected." I had the powerful sensation that, despite my reservations about leaving Buffalo, we'd brought him home.

Jack was very difficult that spring. In his preschool back in Buffalo he'd started biting and kicking both kids and teachers, and everyone seemed at a loss as to how to control his behavior. At home he'd started to hit both Joe and I, and to get into mischief, things like spreading Cool Whip all over his body while I was in the shower, picking the child locks and escaping into the yard, or trying to crawl inside the dishwasher. He was silent and stealthy, a trying combination. We had started some rudimentary means of communication by posting pictures of his favorite items around the house so he could point to things he needed, but still his language was limited to about ten words. In conjunction with his speech therapist and the integrated preschool, Joe and I were doing our best to figure out our enigmatic little boy.

The behaviors continued after we moved, but when we started the BEEP program I felt hopeful for the first time in a very long while. Emily was a bright, energetic young woman with a direct manner and an infectious laugh. Using techniques that alternated between discipline and reward, she reigned in Jack's behavior and counseled us on how to better control him at home. With her firm approach she coaxed language from my son and had him putting two and three words together by the middle of the summer.

In July I gave birth to a girl. We'd always waited until the delivery to learn our child's gender, and I guess we'd both just assumed we were having another boy. I had a similar pregnancy as the first three (though truthfully, I don't know why that would mean anything), so both Joe and I were astounded to discover we now had a daughter. The nurse in the delivery room bent over with laughter, exclaiming, "If I could reach over and tap your husband with my pinky finger, he'd fall right over from shock!" Joe looked almost shaken as he held our latest chubby bundle in his arms. At nine pounds, four ounces, she was our largest baby so far and bore a striking resemblance to the name we'd chosen (just in case), a blooming, pink Rose.

And so we rolled along. Joe's new practice was soon thriving, and I was home with another newborn. Joey and Charlie went to a local preschool a few days a week, and Jack was full-time in Bedford's early education program. Rose was a delightful baby, and I reveled in taking care of what I fully expected to be my last infant. We were all adapting well to New Hampshire and enjoying the closeness of family.

People have sometimes asked me if we ever considered stopping after our second child, given Jack's problems and diagnosis. My answer is always "no." Although several of our pregnancies were surprises, we were always happy to welcome another child. As the youngest of six, Joe had always dreamed of a large family, and he cherished the idea of having kids who were close in age. We certainly considered the possibility that we might have another child with Jack's issues (or worse), but we never dwelled on it. Even now, several years later, I can't explain the momentum that propelled us forward in the face of having a special-needs child. It was simply what we did.

Nonetheless, after Rose we decided we were finished having kids. Four felt like more than enough to me, and although Joe would have gladly welcomed another, he agreed to make an appointment with the urologist for the we're-not-having-another-baby procedure. Not long after we inked the date on our calendar, though, the office called to reschedule because the doctor had a conflict.

Turns out we wouldn't need that appointment for quite a while.

I had been feeling a little off for a few days, and recognized the symptoms well enough to know I needed to take out another one of those little test sticks. When I saw that second pink line, I marched down to where Joe sat working on the computer and indignantly tossed the stick down in front of him. Unable to meet my eyes, he just covered his face and started to laugh.

Nine months later, ten-pound, four-ounce Henry bulldozed his way out of my body and into the world—the equivalent of a human meatball. His feet were so large that the nurse couldn't fit them on the form.

Nothing about this delivery was easy. My water broke at four in the morning—I'm pretty sure Henry punched it open—and when I sat up and asked Joe, "Did you hear that gush?" he ran frantically to the bathroom and brought back exactly one square of toilet paper.

From there began our comedy of errors. For some reason I insisted on taking a shower despite Joe's reminder that my labor always goes very fast once my water breaks. A contraction hit just as I turned the water off and stepped out, so I leaned my fat self on the towel rack for support, and it shattered to the floor. Meanwhile, Joe was trying to get in touch with the babysitter we had prearranged for this occasion, but with no luck reaching her was now attempting to get through to his brother.

On our way to the hospital the pain was so intense that I begged Joe to pull over, but he ignored my pleas and white-knuckled it the rest of the way there. Once in the delivery room, I decided that I was too hot and, in front of everyone, took off every stitch of my clothing. (To this day Joe claims that it seemed like a very natural thing to do at the time.) With no time for an epidural this was my most difficult birth, mostly because I had no experience with hard labor. Luckily it was short, and within twenty minutes Jumbo Henry catapulted into the world.

Shortly after, I reminded Joe that he had a minor procedure to reschedule. This time, the urologist kept the appointment.

Snowflakes ∿

AUTISM SPECTRUM DISORDER affects everyone very differently, and in the eight years since Jack's birth I've never once encountered another person quite like him.

I've spoken with moms who have kids with no language at all, and with parents whose children are astoundingly verbal. Some kids can't tolerate crunchy food; Jack won't touch yogurt or peaches. I once met a teenage boy whose entire diet consisted of four items. There are autistic kids who flap and whirl like dervishes around the room, and others who sit silent and staring, seemingly locked away in their own world. Many shy away from bright light and loud noises, some avoid physical contact altogether. Although bound together by a spectrum disorder diagnosis, autistic people are essentially like snowflakes: all similar yet essentially unique.

Just as autism varies from person to person, it also varies within a person over time. As Jack gets older, his autism changes year by year. Once again I'm reminded of a snow-flake, one inside of him, drifting, melting, and then re-crys-tallizing. Every so often his autism seems to lie dormant for a few minutes, hours, or even a day, and people will remark about how normal he appears. Then, without warning, the snowstorm will begin again.

When Jack was only about ten months old, I sat at the counter at home one day eating lunch and surfing the web when I stumbled across a list detailing the early warning signs of autism in babies and toddlers, things like *doesn't make eye contact* or *doesn't smile when smiled at* or *doesn't use gestures to communicate*. It took my breath away—I had to put my sandwich down and collect myself. It was as though someone had used words to paint a portrait of my son; it described Jack exactly at that point in time. I saved that list, and every now and again I glance at it, remember-ing the baby he was and using it as a checkpoint for the boy he's become. A lot has changed in the seven years since I first found it.

At three, Jack started to make a lot of progress. Settled in the early education program in New Hampshire, he was making great gains in the areas of speech and language. By the end of his first summer in the program, Jack could put two or three words together to form a request and had started to initiate simple games like peek-a-boo or patty-cake. He was potty-trained. We rejoiced in our newfound toddler, a boy who was starting to communicate and play.

And then, nothing. By the fall of 2007 he seemed at a standstill. Even more frustrating were some new behaviors he'd developed. His tantrums picked up, and we had a really hard time getting him to sit for a meal. Dinner time became a war zone as night after night Joe and I would get up from the table to chase Jack down and plant him firmly back in his seat. Emily counseled us to weather these blizzards and that what Jack needed most during these times was our consistency and perseverance. She suggested we set a timer during mealtime so that Jack would understand just how long he had to sit, and, if his tantrums became physical, to hold his hands together firmly but gently and repeat the phrase "quiet body" in order to calm him down.

We moved through this cycle of progress and behavioral problems for the next five years. Jack would make a great leap in one area and then stand nearly motionless for a while before bounding up another riser. And his worst behaviors somehow always emerged right before he took that next step, making it seem as though he were going backwards. When he was five his toileting regressed, and he wet the bed at night. Halfway through first grade he became very explosive at school, screaming and lashing out at other kids. Even now Jack's development never seems to be a steady climb.

As the summer of 2011 began, we met with a new developmental pediatrician to assess Jack's progress and determine an academic strategy for school. Over the course of seven years, Jack had changed so much from that initial list of autism symptoms; he was a different boy entirely.

During our appointment the doctor noted several ways in which Jack differs from the textbook characteristics common to a person on the spectrum. He is extremely affectionate and loving, for example, and can finish my sentences and read nonverbal cues (such as a warning look) from across the room. He prefers a general rhythm to his days but can be more adaptable to change than we sometimes expect, especially if we have time to prepare him for it.

Also, unlike many spectrum kids, Jack is much more comfortable with reading and language than with math. He can solve word problems but struggles when it comes to manipulating numbers for simple addition and subtraction.

Jack and his father play a game together where Joe asks Jack to point to something on the ceiling, and once Jack raises his arm, Joe tickles him. Over time Jack's grown wise, and he keeps his arm close to his side, pointing with only a raised finger and a huge grin on his face. The doctor watched, amazed, as they demonstrated for her. She explained that this type of resourcefulness is rarely found with autism.

On the flip side, Jack has a tendency to do what's called perseverating; he focuses repetitively on random subjects, sometimes for months. At times he's perseverated on cars, license plates, radios, and even what color of shampoo people use. He'll engage with people on these subjects, but even though his eye contact has greatly improved over the years, he is still erratic and unpredictable when meeting someone's gaze. He enjoys being around people, especially our family, but has trouble finding socially appropriate ways to connect with them.

In school he's prone to huge meltdowns and tantrums. He has his own manner of self-stimulation, a key aspect of autism. Self-stimulation, often called "stimming," refers to a repetitive physical behavior people will use to help regulate themselves when faced with a stressful situation. Common self-stimulation practices include things like hand flapping and humming. Jack tends to gallop across the room with his fingers in his mouth and to grunt or loudly clear his throat. We call it his "zoomies." When Jack stims, he looks as though he's possessed, as if someone else has control of his body.

After considering all of this, the doctor recommended neuropsychological testing to get an accurate picture of exactly how Jack thinks and reacts in certain situations. Although officially diagnosed with Pervasive Developmental Disorder, Not Otherwise Specified (PDD-NOS) in 2005, we hadn't explored any other kinds of tests since then. Now that Jack could communicate more effectively, we'd begun to notice that he really does see the world very differently from us and that perhaps we would have more success tapping into that fascinating mind if we understood it better.

Our psychologist performed the testing over the course of the next two months. One morning a week I would bring Jack to her office and wait in the lobby while she took him through a series of questions and games, trying to get a peek inside his complicated mind. Then I would drag him to school (sometimes kicking and screaming because he wanted to go home). A few weeks after the testing, we were provided with a twenty-five page report.

Much of Jack's issues, it turns out, are related to sensory integration and his own internal regulation. The abbreviated clinical version of the report says that Jack struggles with regulation, cognitive flexibility, working memory and processing, and auditory and visual complexity.

Last winter we decided to take the kids to see a holiday light show at a nearby race track. On the day of the show we'd taken Jack out of school for a doctor's appointment and treated him to lunch afterwards. Joe and I had enjoyed our special afternoon alone with him, and our entire family was in a festive mood as we headed out for dinner and the show. But on the way to the restaurant Jack overheard his two brothers talking about the all-school meeting they'd attended that day, and Jack quickly became extremely agitated because he loves all-school meetings. Jack *lives* for all-school meetings. And he was very, very angry he had missed one.

He started screaming and banging his head, saying things like "I hate school! I hate my friends who went to the meeting without me!" On the car ride to dinner he alternated between trying to jump out of his seat and saying he wanted to throw up. Somewhat mystified by this reaction, Joe and I decided to go ahead with the evening as planned, hoping Jack would become distracted and calm back down.

He continued to rage and seethe even after we were all seated in the restaurant. His body was in such turmoil that he couldn't sit still. He wouldn't touch his food, and finally I took him to the car to try and calm both his body and his mind, but I had no luck. I probed to try and find out just why these meetings were so important to him, why he felt so insulted. I reminded him of the pleasant afternoon we'd enjoyed together, of how there would be several more all-school meetings in the spring. Nothing would calm him.

Joe finished dinner with the other kids and brought them all back to the car. Caught up in the holiday gaiety, they'd overlooked Jack's tantrum and were excited to see the lights. Not for the first time, Joe and I felt trapped between managing the demands of autism and keeping the rest of our family happy. We decided to soldier on to the race track, thinking that maybe the visual distraction would be enough to help Jack regulate himself.

As I look back on this memory, I realize now that he was too far gone, that his internal system was too out of sorts for him to regain control. As we wound slowly through the track of lights, the other kids stood in the van nibbling candy canes and pointing out the assortment of elves, reindeer, and trees to each other. Jack huddled in the backseat, gesturing wildly to himself and speaking incoherent sentences in frantic tones.

For the entire ride home he ranted and railed, waging his own verbal war against school meetings, his friends, and even his brothers. Once home he started to wind down from sheer exhaustion, finally falling asleep with tears on his cheeks.

Deregulated.

Although he doesn't seem to have problems with things like tags on his shirts or clothing in general, any kind of change to his body is difficult for Jack to manage. As soon as he feels a loosening tooth, he begs my husband to pull it out. He's driven to distraction by the sensation of it wobbling around. Something like a stuffy nose or a hang nail can ruin his day.

Bowel movements are especially challenging. Many days Jack races off the bus and rushes into the house to use the bathroom, and sometimes he'll spend half an hour rocking and groaning as he tries to make himself comfortable. Often he takes off all of his clothes and makes a tremendous mess of himself. It is very stressful for both of us.

Sounds often contribute to Jack's deregulation as well. Like with many on the spectrum, he struggles with what specialists sometimes refer to as auditory complexity. Back when he was in second grade, Jack refused to sit at the reading table during class and listen to his peers read their parts of the assignment. Once Jack himself had finished reading he became antsy and uncomfortable, begging to return to his own desk. After observing him, our psychologist suggested that Jack has a low tolerance for repetitive noise and the rhythmic sound of six second-graders reading aloud one after another just drove him crazy.

Jack can't seem to determine if a sound is a foreground

or background noise, and he's easily distracted by something like a passing car. Too many words or commands overwhelm him, and he's unable to hold onto information long enough to work with it in his memory. Because of this, he can't process directions or conversations that last longer than one or two minutes.

When I'm giving directions to all five children, say at the dinner table or in the car, Jack will often interrupt me with a loud "What—what—what?" and I know that I'm talking too quickly and he can't keep up. (In fact, this happens so much throughout the day that sometimes when Joe and I come downstairs together after putting the kids to bed, one of us will look at the other and say "What—what—what?" before cracking up. Sometimes you just have to laugh.)

Jack's limited working memory results in significant communication challenges. In his mind words are as slippery as falling snowflakes, and as quickly as he grabs hold of one idea, another one slides out of his cerebral grasp. When he's asked a question it's as though he has to mentally bend down and retrieve that one idea out of many, re-examine it, and figure out if it's what he needs. It takes him a while to answer.

Because he works so hard to manage information, Jack tends to socially engage with people using familiar topics. He spent the better part of a school year asking all the kids how many radios they had because he could quickly organize a response to their answer. If the conversation continued beyond the number and color of their radio, things got trickier for him. He appeared to lose interest and wander off, but really he couldn't process the new information or respond spontaneously to it.

He's also a literal thinker and has trouble with cognitive flexibility and theory of mind. An aspect of social cognition, theory of mind is the ability to understand that others have beliefs, opinions, and feelings different than your own. Jack, however, thinks everyone sees and feels and likes the same things he does. A few months ago a new restaurant opened in our town, and one Friday night we all went there for dinner. The kids were thrilled to discover they had corn dogs on the menu. The following Friday Jack asked if we could go back to the restaurant so he could have the corn dog again. We agreed, and once seated in the restaurant he took all the kids' menus at our table and circled the corn dog option for each of them in bright red crayon. "We're all getting corn dogs!" he gleefully exclaimed, disregarding Rose's protest for a hamburger and Henry's cries for pizza. As an inflexible thinker, Jack couldn't understand that anyone at our table could even consider something other than what he was longing for: a corn dog.

Jack's internal demands are more compelling than most; he has trouble integrating his inside world with the external world around him. As a result, he will sometimes give in to what he wants to do, what he thinks he has to do, even if he knows it's not what I want.

One day during winter break he and his siblings built an

40

elaborate fort in the playroom using blankets, sheets, and pillows. Delighted with their space, they all begged to sleep there for the rest of school vacation. During the third night of their new sleeping arrangements, however, the shine wore off, and one by one they got up and returned to their own (more comfortable) beds.

The next morning I folded umpteen blankets and returned various pillow pets and assorted slippers to their rightful rooms. On my way out to yoga I reminded Jack that we weren't sleeping there anymore and to leave the room clean. I left the kids with a sitter for about two hours and came home to find the playroom in complete disarray again. Jack had taken out what seemed like every single blanket and pillow we owned, piling them atop bean bags, chairs, and even inside a small tent. He had dragged most of the smaller furniture into the center of the room, built elaborate "walls" with cardboard blocks, and balanced the trampoline on its side to make a makeshift steering wheel. (Don't ask me why a fort needs a steering wheel. I don't know.) My voice choked with frustration as I asked him why he had pulled everything out when I had just put it all away. He simply said that he wanted to sleep in the playroom again.

I knew he understood my earlier instructions about the room staying clean, and deep down I also knew that his intent wasn't to disobey me. He can't always balance his own internal wants with the external demands of others. I could only sigh and begin—one more time—to clean up the room.

Today, Jack's issues are much different than the early

days of *doesn't smile when smiled at* and *won't look at me*, and I know the future will bring an entirely different set of challenges. Capturing Jack's autism is a lot like capturing a snowflake on the tip of your finger. The moment you're close enough to understand and admire its fragile beauty, it changes into something else entirely.

Making Progress: Stretch, Don't Break ໑

IN OUR EARLY DAYS WITH AUTISM, back when Jack was a chubby, blue-eyed toddler, much of our daily lives revolved around encouraging him to speak and keeping him engaged. When he was about a year old we started using sign language for simple commands like "more" and "all done," and we would work steadily at having him look us in the eyes in order to create connection.

When he was just under two, we made pictures of his favorite foods and toys. We posted them all over the house so he could point to what he wanted instead of screaming. One of Joe's fondest memories is of Jack walking to the refrigerator, pointing to a picture of Cheerios in a snack cup, and pretending to eat them. It was a Cheerio breakthrough; Jack was identifying the food and engaging in pretend play.

Once he did start speaking consistently (at around the age of three), we constantly encouraged him to use his words. I distinctly remember tapping my lips with my forefinger over and over, asking him to "Say it. Say cookie, Jack. Say it." A behavioral therapist warned us to be careful about anticipating his needs; instead we should give him the chance to articulate what he wanted, even if it meant building time into our routine to accommodate his pace. She suggested giving him choices throughout the day so he could exercise and grow his vocabulary.

Say it.

In addition to language, we were always trying to get him to look us in the eye. Another popular line in our growing repertoire of commands was "Look at me." Whenever I spoke to him, I would kneel down to his level and place my fingers on his chin to connect his gaze with mine. We named things for him incessantly, pointing with an exaggerated gesture to direct his attention.

Mama. Dada. Cup. Bird.

After a while, every interaction with little Jack began to feel deliberate, orchestrated toward some faraway goal. I complained one day to our speech therapist that with Jack nothing felt spontaneous, every one of his actions had a reaction, and every nuance of his behavior was recorded and examined. "It will," she soothed. "You'll see how much easier this will get."

Sometimes it didn't feel worth it. It didn't feel like repeating "Look in my eyes" a hundred times a day could possibly release this little boy from his inner sanctum, or that sign language would ever lead to actual words coming out of his precious mouth. Sometimes I just wanted to let him watch those *Baby Einstein* movies he loved so much, to be and let be.

And sometimes I did.

But for the most part, we were consistent in our efforts to draw him out and pull him toward us. We stretched ourselves, and little by little, it paid off; like a baby bird cracking out of his shell, two-year-old Jack slowly broke through his silence and began to chirp. He'd always been very affectionate and physical, but his affections became more directed and focused. It felt as though he'd joined our family at last.

His neurological test results presented a whole new set of both obstacles and goals for our eight-year-old son. Reading about his issues with things like regulation and cognitive flexibility made me panic. How could we ever take all of this information and package it so that we had a plan of attack? Jack's issues seemed so widespread; could we really teach him to move the sound of a siren to the back of his brain and to concentrate on his spelling instead? How do you increase a person's theory of mind and help them understand that others think and feel differently? We'd moved from reminding him to make eye contact and noticing a squirrel outside the window to trying to teach him that he can handle the way a loose tooth feels in his mouth.

I was overwhelmed.

With the help of our psychologist, we took the lengthy report bullet by bullet, problem by problem, and created a strategy to address each of Jack's challenges. The idea was to increase his ability in each of the identified areas—self-regulation, communication, and cognitive ability. Essentially, we wanted Jack to learn to stretch himself like a rubber band but also to have the skills he needed to identify his breaking point before he snapped.

I started to observe his regulation more closely and took note of when his body seemed calm and his mind more open (as opposed to his looking and feeling distressed). One winter I enrolled the boys in ski and snowboarding lessons, and every Monday, after an hour of snowboarding, one thing was clear: Jack's body felt good. On the car ride home he was present, engaged, and peaceful. He joked and laughed with his brothers; one week he even developed a game for finishing homework and explained it to them. I began to notice the correlation between his level of physical activity and his ability to participate in the world around him.

Jack adapts to his surroundings and learns best when his body feels ready, when the ants of self-stimulation are quiet and his mind is calm. Exercise and movement are essential for him to feel regulated. Now, if we notice he has the "zoomies" and needs to stim, we direct him toward the mini-trampoline in the playroom or to his bike outside. If the weather's good we'll try to squeeze in a few scooter rides down our long driveway before school in the morning. Once at school, they have him perform things like wall push-ups and jumping jacks if he seems deregulated.

Our psychologist advised that the trick is to get Jack to notice his body's arousal before it hits what we sometimes call his "red zone," the place where he's past the point of no return, like on the evening of the holiday light show. She suggested using a program called "How Does Your Engine Run?" First developed back in 1996, the approach specifically targets ways to help children minimize deregulation by paying attention to their bodies. At school Jack made a small booklet identifying how his body feels and what the appropriate activity would be in response. It's attached to a keychain, and he keeps it with him throughout the day.

I try to ask him how his engine feels a few times a day, getting him to label the sensations he's experiencing. One time he was in a rage because I told him he'd had enough marshmallows for the day, and then I added insult to injury by asking him in that exact moment how his engine felt.

"Mad and hungry!"

I asked him what he could do about that, hoping he would solve his own problem, perhaps by jumping on the trampoline. Nope.

"Eat another marshmallow!"

Another time he was snuggled up in front of the fireplace watching one of his beloved *Baby Einstein* videos, surrounded by assorted stuffed animals and brothers. His face looked relaxed, and his body was limp. I asked him how his engine felt.

"Just right."

As important as it is for Jack to stay calm, it's just as important for the adults in his world to remain composed. When he gets aroused, it's very tempting for me to mirror his distress, raise my voice, and meet him in the red zone. Now I force myself to keep it together, and sometimes I even repeat "just right" to myself—my job is to get him to feel "just right."

Jack's communication issues are twofold: he struggles with both expressing himself and with receiving complex verbal information. Each of these are further compromised when he's in a stressful situation or if he's deregulated. I wish there was an easy fix for his communication problems, that something as concrete as jumping on a trampoline could produce tangible results, but that's not always enough. Instead, Joe and I have incorporated our psychologist's concept of "low and slow" into our parenting approach.

Low and slow means pretty much what it says; keep your voice low and your words slow. This was not an intuitive way for me to communicate with my kids, by the way; I prefer the "high and fast" method myself. It's taken a fair amount of practice for me to slow down and lower my voice when I'm agitated. All of us are slowly stretching.

Luckily, our larger family gives Jack a lot of opportunity to spontaneously interact. Unaware of his specific communication problems, his siblings expect answers when they ask Jack a question and all but demand his participation in their play. Six-year-old Charlie is especially adept at drawing Jack out.

"Jack, I asked you if you want milk or juice. Milk or juice?"

I do have to remind the kids to keep it low and slow for Jack, to give him time to listen and respond. Basically we all have to accept his limitations and give him the space to flex his mind.

In school Jack receives speech therapy twice a week. At this point they're focusing on improving his conversation skills and social communication. Also, one day a week he selects a friend to join him back in the classroom for "lunch bunch," a time for them to enjoy a quiet meal together and to give Jack a chance to work on his peer-interaction skills.

And for those moments when Jack's in the red zone and simply can't find the words, we've worked with his team to create visual tools to aid him. At school he has a thermometer with different temperature zones to indicate how he feels in a heated moment. Helping him label his internal temperature will hopefully lead to greater emotional competence and increase his ability to tolerate certain feelings for longer periods of time.

A few months ago I was proudly telling our psychologist about how Jack had been making breakfast for Joey before school each morning. To my delight, sometimes I'd come downstairs and find two identical bowls of cereal and cups of juice arranged at the counter.

I was pleased with both his initiative and independence, but she gently reminded me that it's also a sign of his limited theory of mind: he assumed Joey wanted the same meal he did. (Luckily, Joey is pretty flexible.) In an effort to stretch his cognitive ability, she suggested we have him ask his brother what he'd like to eat. Now we have a game we play called "Waiter" where he takes a pen and paper and asks everyone in the house what they're in the mood for. (Note: this can backfire. Charlie once asked for shrimp lo mein for lunch. He got peanut butter and jelly instead.)

We try and work in small cognitive exercises like this throughout our day. They encourage Jack to notice how the people around him might think or feel. One night his older brother was ticked off because we'd told him to shut off the Wii and go to bed. As Joey stomped around the playroom I turned to Jack and asked, "How does Joey feel now?" He answered, "Mad! No more Wii!" He followed it up with "I'll play it instead," and I watched as Joey hit the red zone this time.

I guess his theory of mind is improving.

Since Jack has trouble managing too much auditory noise at once, we've learned to give brief, concise directions like "Get milk please" or "Put shoes on." Since I have a tendency to over-explain my instructions, this has meant a new habit for me; before I might have told Jack something like "Could you please get me more milk out of the refrigerator? We need it for cereal." He would've stopped listening at "refrigerator," and when I saw he was tuning out, I'd start the whole dialogue over again, taking it even further: "You want cereal, don't you? Aren't you hungry? You need to eat to have a good day!" I'd be rewarded with a blank, empty stare.

Get milk. Please.

(Note: direct communication seems to work with all of my kids. They respond faster and understand instructions better. I guess I was just talking too much before.)

We're trying to help Jack understand that there are multiple ways of solving a problem or completing a task—this will hopefully help him to become a more flexible thinker. We brainstorm about different ways we can spend our afternoon, for example, or if time allows, I'll sometimes take a different route home so that Jack sees that there's more than one path to travel.

We've also introduced what are called "social stories" into Jack's routine to help better prepare him for an unexpected event or transition. A social story basically describes a situation and explains what is expected from each individual within the story. They're kind of like mini-instruction manuals for unfamiliar events, written from Jack's perspective. At home we've used them to help explain things like how to behave during a party or what is involved in a trip to the library. At school they use them to help him prepare for events like a fire drill or an early dismissal. Sometimes I create the social stories on the computer and use pictures to demonstrate my expectations. An abbreviated version looks like this :

Today our family is going to the library. I will bring my book with me and return it in the wooden slot when

we get there. It is very quiet in the library, and I must
whisper. After I return my book I can choose a new one
to bring home. The librarian will check me out.

Every year Jack is evaluated for his Individual Education
Plan (IEP), a document that describes his individual social
and academic goals and any additional support he might
require (such as a shared or full-time aide, occupational
therapy, or speech therapy). We utilized the results of the
neuropsychological testing to add important pieces into his
IEP and school day.

Jack, integrated into a mainstream kindergarten classroom, shares an aide with another student and receives occupational therapy and speech services twice a week, usually
outside of the classroom. Occupational therapy (OT) covers
a wide range of skills; Jack's therapist works with him on
fine motor challenges such as handwriting and pencil grip,
as well as sensory integration and regulation. She gives him
strategies to keep his body calm when he's deregulated, like
those wall push-ups or jumping jacks (a term that never fails
to make him giggle).

His speech therapy also covers a broad range of topics,
ranging from articulation and vocabulary, to reading facial
expressions and understanding dialogue. In addition, they've
built in social goals like his "lunch bunch," that once-a-week
chance to selects friends to share lunchtime in the classroom.
His aide orchestrates conversation and discussion between

the students so Jack can get a chance to learn appropriate exchanges in a smaller setting.

There was no question in my mind that all of these strategies and techniques and new habits were helping. But were they helping enough? After a few months I felt like I was again at the same crossroad as when Jack was three. Can little games like "Waiter" really help Jack understand that others have thoughts and feelings, too? Some days it feels like reminding Jack to jump on the trampoline is pointless in the looming face of autism. But then I take a deep breath and remember: that's life with a special needs kiddo. Every day you have to show up, stand up, and stretch without breaking.

My Paper Boy ❧

I HAVE AN ENORMOUS BLUE FOLDER labeled "Jack" that's crammed full of early intervention evaluations, IEP reports, and now, neuropsychological test results. Dating back to before his first birthday, this paperwork chronicles everything from Jack's ability to hear, to when he first started stringing two words together. It's all too easy—and sad—to see him reduced to just the information in this blue folder, to a set of symptoms and limitations and issues.

The paper version of Jack shows that he was born on May 9, 2004. At eight years of age, he stands 53″ tall and weighs 62 pounds. His sneaker is a size five. His eyes are a grayish-blue, and he has light brown hair (usually worn in a crew cut because he can't stand having it combed). His left pupil is larger than his right, the result of a harmless congenital condition known as Horner's Syndrome.

On paper, Jack is diagnosed with autism.

His diagnosis says he has limited verbal skills, makes variable eye contact, and lacks sociability. He engages in obsessive behavior and has difficulty interpreting social cues from those around him.

I remember attending Jack's very first IEP meeting in Buffalo, New York, and listening to the entire group of therapists and teachers refer to him as "child."

"Child has limited verbal skills," said one.

"Child needs visual cues to communicate," offered another.

"Child is self-directed," added a third.

It went on and on until I wanted to light each one of my eyelashes on fire and dart from the room. But what I wanted to do even more was shriek things like "His name is Jack! He is two years old! He's really cute! And he loves Cool Whip!" From that point forward I resolved to never reduce Jack to a mere paper boy, but instead to spring him to life in all of his autistic glory, to really see him for who he is. Because underneath all of the diagnostic testing and medical terminology was a beautiful, sweet little boy struggling to shine. Behind the relentless stimming, the horrific tantrums, and—perhaps worst of all—the silence, was my Jack.

As his mother, it's my job to make sure the world sees him, too.

A paper explanation doesn't begin to describe what his diagnosis means in everyday life. As a toddler, Jack used to laugh uncontrollably at a particular *Baby Einstein* video, and he became attached to a stuffed bunny—named Bunny—that he still sleeps with today. His first word was "ball," and it came shortly before his second birthday. From very early on he was capable of sly—very sly—manipulation ("Mommy, a cookie feels my throat better").

He threw enormous tantrums and would often rage until someone in the house figured out, for example, that he wanted juice. This could take up to forty-five minutes, draw countless tears from several people, and result in a lot of refrigerator banging. Jack also doesn't always appear to listen when someone is talking to him, so we spend a fair amount of time commanding him to look us in the eye when we speak. As a baby he could spend endless time tracing the same grout line over and over again, or he might just stare off into space for long periods. People make him nervous, and he struggles to interpret facial expressions. He loves to ask questions like "How old are you?" and follow it up with the zinger, "And when do you think you're going to die?" oblivious to his squirming subject's red-faced sputtering. Apparently people don't like to have their mortality questioned by a child.

When we moved to New Hampshire in April 2007, I was relieved to discover his new team was warm and loving. In our very first meeting together they asked to see a picture of him, and "Child" was replaced by "Jack." Together we laughed over his quirks and looked hopefully towards his year in a new preschool. At last, people who could see beyond the paper boy.

Jack's paper diagnosis fails to capture the beautiful gifts

of his autism. He seems to have a heightened sense of hearing which allows him to perceive the slightest difference in sound and music, and he has a remarkable memory with an uncanny capacity to retain information. Just last week he and I were in Walgreens, where we both noticed a mother toting a newborn in an infant car seat. We took a peek, and as I chatted with the mom about the baby's name and age, Jack asked what day she was born. The woman told him the baby's birthday was February 21, and without hesitation Jack responded, "Oh. This baby was born on a Thursday." He then matter-of-factly moved on to the gum display while she and I gaped.

One day last fall he asked me, "What color do you see for Monday?" as I heaved a chicken into the oven. "What?" I said distractedly, turning from the oven to slice some potatoes at the counter. It was late afternoon, and I was preparing dinner and managing the demands of homework and tired toddlers. "Do you see days as colors?"

"Yes. All days are colors."

All days are colors. In one seemingly ordinary moment, Jack once again granted me the privilege to take a tiny peek inside his fascinating mind. Without preamble, he rattled off which color he associates with each day. Then, just as suddenly as the conversation began, he snapped his mind closed and moved on to something else entirely. I tried to probe further. "Why was Tuesday green?" I wanted to know. "Was the entire day green, or just the morning?"

"I told you. No more," he responded in a clipped tone.

Jack loves pancakes and is a great bowler. He's very proud of riding the big bus to school and is soothed by music, especially anything by Rihanna or Katy Perry. Although he loves music, he rarely sings out loud. We nicknamed him Jack-a-boo or Kangaroo Jack because of the way he bounces through the room when he's stimming.

None of this shows up anywhere in that blue folder.

Jack's paper version makes me feel sad, terrified, and anxious. I'm sometimes angered by his limitations and because he wasn't born normal, and I'm afraid of the long, unknown road ahead of us. I'm concerned he'll need to live with us forever.

But my real-life Jack makes me feel hopeful, hopeful that he can overcome some of the obstacles his autism presents and make a life for himself. Although sometimes I'm anxious that he'll never live independently, I'm also inspired by how hard he works. And I'm fascinated by his unique mind. I am lucky to know him.

Sometimes I start to panic when I think about his issues and our future, and then it's easy for me to diminish my son to his paper version. Frequent school meetings and trips to the developmental pediatrician are all-too-painful reminders of his strengths and weaknesses, spelled out for us in black and white. But as I remind myself when the words start to swim up and take the shape of my actual real-life boy, autism is a diagnosis, and that's all. Although it's as much a part of Jack as the two freckles on his face and his love of Scooby Doo, it's just one mere aspect of his whole extraordinary being.

He's beautiful inside, outside, and even on paper.

When We Can't Find the Words ∾

"BECAUSE I WANT TO!" Jack screamed, stomping his foot and punching the air with balled-up fists.

Joe's sister got married last summer, and the day before her wedding we hosted a big barbecue at our house for the entire family. Between grandparents, aunts, uncles, and cousins, we had over forty people watching Jack's defiant tantrum.

He wanted to eat up in the playroom. Several times I looked over to see him creeping up the stairs, holding a red plastic plate piled high with cocktail meatballs and cheese. And several times I walked up to him, took the plate away, and reminded him that we only eat in the kitchen, especially with the brand-new carpet we'd just installed up there. Each time, his patience (and mine) wore thinner and thinner. He started to rage, and the last struggle was a tug-of-war between us that ended with an overturned plate on the floor.

Needless to say, I was very, very frustrated. Jack knows the rules of our house and, for the most part, respects them. I couldn't figure out why he thought today was an exception, why he thought he could eat where he pleased. And tomato-sauced meatballs, of all things!

I tried to block out the soothing voices behind me. "What does it matter? It's a party!" "Let him eat where he wants!" "He's overwhelmed!" Gritting my teeth, I took Jack firmly by the arm and marched him off for a break.

He *was* overwhelmed, that much was obvious. We were on our third day of out-of-town company and wedding festivities and were all feeling a little threadbare from late nights and busy days. I brought Jack to my room, along with Bunny, his favorite stuffed animal. Before I switched on the television I asked him again why he wanted to eat up in the playroom.

"Because. I want to."

After a few episodes of Scooby Doo he calmed down and the rest of the afternoon went smoothly. He didn't try again to eat anywhere but in the kitchen, and I thought it was just a case of overstimulation and exhaustion.

But the following Monday morning, when the wedding vows and music and dancing were over, when the guests were gone and our house had returned to normal, I walked him down the driveway to catch the bus for camp. And without preamble he asked me, "How come cousins can eat in the playroom?"

Ahhh.

A light bulb went off, and I realized the reason he had so badly wanted to drag his plate up there. He'd seen his older cousins enjoying their meal and wanted to join them. I was sad. Sad that I'd made a spectacle of him, sad that he had wanted to join his family socially and I'd stood in his way, sad that I'd made those stupid meatballs because maybe I could have overlooked something innocuous, like chicken fingers.

Later that week we had an appointment with our developmental pediatrician. Sitting in her tiny office with Joe, I tearfully relayed the events of the weekend. She explained to us how the skills we each work the hardest to gain are the ones we lose first in a stressful situation. Amidst the chaos and commotion, Jack just couldn't reach for the words to explain why it was so important for him to eat in the playroom. Several days later he was regulated enough to tell us what he was thinking.

I wondered what I could do to avoid this sort of thing in the future. She suggested that I think quickly and assess the situation before acting. This sort of patience is the exact skill I work the hardest on — and the first one to go when I'm under stress. An excerpt of my notes from that appointment looks like this:

The skill we work the hardest for is the one we lose first under stress. (For Jack: communication—for me: patience.)

Always assume for all of the kids that behavior has a purpose—this is VERY BIG!! (E.g., Jack was getting up from the table last night because he wanted to refill his cup.)

Try to figure out what problem could be causing his stress—anything physical (headache, hangnail, gas)?

Stand back and think of all the options first. Keep it low and slow, low and slow, low and slow.

Sometimes words do come to Jack, but they are the wrong words.

He became very, very agitated in school one day and blurted out, "I want to kill everyone!" Living as we do in a post-Columbine world, a phrase like this is not taken lightly—even from an autistic second-grader. They whisked him out of the classroom and up to the office, where he was visited by the vice principal. By the time he had received a stern talking-to, Jack was shaking and nauseous.

Later I read about the turn of events in his daily notebook. I was sad again because I could picture him blurting out those words in the middle of a rage, with little appreciation for their meaning. Sad because at times he's so misunderstood.

Did Jack learn a lesson from the vice principal's lecture? Probably not. In some future moment of panic and fury he will probably shout out another taboo phrase.

Jack's language can be very abrasive and at times borders on being offensive. He's been known to walk into the kitchen and demand "Get me my breakfast now!" or to tell me "Don't you dare pack more of those white cookies!" as I put his school lunch together.

He feels things very intensely, and his communications mirror his passion. For example, Jack is never just hungry. He's so hungry he's "going to DIE!" And after he's eaten, instead of simply saying he's full, sometimes he starts to jump around and shout, "I have too much food! I'm going to throw up now!" We're usually a big hit in restaurants.

In second grade Jack had to make an entry in a journal every day, based on a topic given by his teacher. He hated this assignment. His teacher sent the journal home every month so we could take a look at it. The following is an excerpt from one week in September:

9/5/2011—I hate my journal.

9/6/2011—Journals are stupid.

9/7/2011—I want to throw my journal in the garbige.

9/8/2011—Journals make me want to throw up.

9/9/2011—I'm going to rip this journal into peeses.

You get the picture. This went on for months, until, shortly after the December break, Jack fell head-over-heels in love with a girl in his class, Isabella. Then his journal read like this:

1/9/2012—I love Isabella.

1/10/2012—She is pretty. I will marry her.

1/11/2012—I like Isabella. I love Isabella.

1/12/2012—Isabella and I will get marryd.

1/13/2012—Isabella is so pretty.

On one occasion Jack became angry with Isabella because she didn't sit with him at lunch. That day his entry said, "Next year Isabella isn't getting any presents for Christmas." Hell hath no fury like Jack when he's scorned.

For the longest time Jack would say things like "I want to eat my friends. I want them in my belly." We were completely bewildered by these phrases, and he'd repeat them upwards of twenty times a day. At last it dawned on us that he wanted to keep his friends close, that this odd expression was a way for him to say he cared about them.

During his year in kindergarten, Jack spent mornings with the mainstream class and afternoons with Miss Nancy, a special education teacher. She worked with him for the entire school year, constantly fielding questions about what color her shampoo was, how many radios she had, and when she celebrated her birthday. Jack was happy in her class and gained a number of new skills during that time.

Fast-forward two years. Joe has the three older boys in Lowes, and they run into Miss Nancy. The moment he sees her, Jack hides his face in his hands and won't meet her gaze. For a few minutes she tries to get him to talk to her, to say hello. Finally he raises his head and, with his eyes lowered, quietly murmurs, "Miss Nancy. I've missed you."

For two long years he'd never once mentioned her. It

made me wonder what other memories he might have, memories he can't find the words to describe.

In Walgreens recently, he kept trying to redirect me to the aisle with markers and crayons. Since we have about forty zillion markers at home already, I firmly told him we weren't buying any more. To signal my resolve, I walked out of the aisle and towards the cash register, leaving him behind. He started to shout, "Help! I'm lost! My mother has left me!"

(Funny how sometimes he *can* find the words, isn't it? Shall we say it together? *Ma-nip-u-la-tion.*)

I raced back to get him and reiterated that we were not buying markers. "Please. I need them. For Mrs. Thaler." I tried to ask why, why he thought Mrs. Thaler wanted the markers, but he wouldn't answer. I had no idea why Jack thought he needed to buy school supplies for his second-grade teacher, but I remembered the conversation with the developmental pediatrician and summoned up the spirit of "every behavior has a reason." I let him get them. (Plus, Henry had been up all night with croup, and I was too tired to argue about Crayola products any longer.)

As soon as we got home, Jack raced to the closet and took out pink wrapping paper covered with dancing princesses. As Joe and I exchanged glances and I-don't-get-it-either shrugs, Jack dragged out scissors and tape, wrapped the eight-pack of classic color markers, and stowed them in his backpack. The next day he gave them to his beloved Mrs. Thaler.

I ran into her a few weeks later and asked how she had liked her gift. She explained how touched she was, because a few days prior she'd called down to the office to request more markers. The person in the office announced over the classroom loudspeaker that she'd have to wait; they were currently out of them.

I am trying, trying to stop and take a moment when it seems like Jack's requesting something out of the ordinary to figure out what's underneath. To presume his behavior has a purpose.

Recently we were all stuck in the house on a rainy Sunday afternoon, and during nap time I stole a quiet moment to write. As I worked in the office that sits just off of our family room, I could see Jack heading toward me carrying a plate that held a large, gooey cupcake and several cookies. I gently reminded him that we don't bring food into the family room, and he put his head down and slunk back towards the kitchen, only to reappear again and again, plate in hand. He finally burst out with "This is a snack! For you! You like cupcakes!" Regretfully I realized that he had assembled the little dish of treats for me to enjoy while I worked.

I guess you could say we're both still learning.

Cookies for Dad ❧

I HAD A MOMENT'S PAUSE recently as I watched my husband Joe pass by me into our family room to hand our daughter her favorite pink blanket and then settle in to snuggle with all five kids on the couch. He looked like the same college guy I met when he was twenty and I just nineteen. Yet over the course of more than a decade we've built a life together based on love, family, and, for the past eight years, autism.

Like all parents, Joe and I don't always see eye-to-eye when it comes to managing our kids. With five little ones between the ages of three and nine, tension is unavoidable. And things can get really fun when you throw a child with autism into the mix.

Statistics show that divorce is on the rise for couples in general, with a higher rate for parents raising a child on the spectrum. Trying to navigate a world full of acronyms while handling the daily behavioral challenges of a kiddo who throws massive tantrums, stims through the room like a cyclone, and tries to start the family minivan if you don't hide the keys can wear down even the happiest couple.

Joe and I have been deliberate about keeping our marriage successful in the midst of five small children, a busy career in dentistry, and day-to-day life. Soon after Joey was born we instituted a weekly date night and have stuck with it ever since. We've been very practical about making sure we stay connected, keeping open communication, and (for the most part) respecting each other's parenting. (This translates into the don't-ever-contradict-me-in-front-of-the-kids rule.)

Still, raising our crew doesn't always bring out the best in us. There are moments of incredible stress—like when the baby has an exploding diaper and another child wants to eat his millionth candy bar—all while we're on display at the annual family reunion down in New Jersey. We'll still sometimes butt heads over things like whether or not we think Jack's ready to start attending church or if he should get a reprieve from eating all of his squash at dinner (since Jack thinks that "Squash is bad for me and will make me sick"). Being a parent is never easy and never quite what we expected. Autism simply adds a whole new dimension.

And it's so easy to vilify the husband. In many families the man gets to trot off to work and leave the domestic mess in the rearview mirror for the day. I remember waking up to Jack's deep nasal whine when we lived in Buffalo and thinking, "I simply cannot get through another day of this." (We nicknamed him Tuggy because his constant whimpering sounded just like the horn of a tugboat.) There's no way that Joe's day—complete with cavity fillings and teeth whitenings—could possibly compare with keeping Jack (and the other small children we have) happy. Never mind that the guy would often find himself walking into a beehive when he got home—with Queen Bee herself in the foulest of moods.

But at the end of even the worst day, Joe is my partner in the long, sometimes lonely road of parenting a spectrum child. In-laws try to be supportive and friends do their best to understand, but my husband has been with me since the moment this nine-pound, three-ounce boy first arrived. Together we've experienced the bumpy ride through Jack's earliest years, as we waited with bated breath for sounds to emerge from this wordless child. Together we felt the icy fingers of fear gripping our hearts and heard the persistent voices in our heads chanting *something is wrong with him, something is wrong with him, something is wrong with him.* Together we accepted the news of his diagnosis and looked toward our new future with a mixture of trepidation and optimism.

Between those reflux and respiratory issues, Jack was a fussy baby and a terrible sleeper. Night after night Joe rocked him through those painful ear infections while I rested. After each feeding he would swaddle Jack in a light blue blanket and hold him tightly on his lap in an effort to calm Jack's painful indigestion.

Things have certainly gotten easier in many ways since

those early days. Jack communicates better now, keeps a regular sleeping schedule, and has the services he needs to keep him progressing. The focus of our parenting has shifted from keeping him comfortable and happy to balancing out how we push him further while still respecting the limits of his autism.

When Jack was in kindergarten, Joe walked him down our long driveway to catch the bus each morning. On the first day of school he started a routine where he would wave to Jack through the window and call out, "Bye Jack! I love you!" as the bus pulled away. Every single day, from the first muggy morning in August, through a bright crisp fall, and all through the snowy winter and muddy spring, Joe repeated his farewell, hopeful that once, just once, Jack would look out the window and wave back. It wasn't until May—nearly the end of the school year—that Joe walked back into the house misty-eyed to tell me that Jack had finally peered through the grimy window and mouthed "Good-bye, Daddy. Love you!"

Today, Joe's calm and logical voice always steps in just when I'm ready to give in and give up, to throw in the towel on yet another battle over putting on gloves or finishing homework.

One summer we visited a zoo in Maine with my brother, his wife, and their infant daughter. We created a social story to prepare Jack for this event, chronicling all the animals we might see, the dinner we would have, how he needed to behave. We broached the subject with Jack two days earlier, and he seemed positive about the whole idea. "Zoos! Zoos are fun!" he exclaimed heartily. His attitude changed radically when our minivan rolled into the parking lot. He started to scream and beat his hands on his head to some mysterious internal rhythm. As we unloaded and shuttled everyone — four adults, five children, and a baby — toward the entrance, Jack's distress visibly increased and he started shouting, "No animals! No animals!"

Again, it was Joe who calmly sat with Jack for nearly half an hour, methodically explaining that the animals stay in their cages and how the zoo is safe. He suggested that they hold hands as they walked through the exhibits. By the end of our trip, Jack was racing the others to be the first one at the tiger cage.

Now that is a father's dedication.

We braved our small town's fireworks display this past Fourth of July, and I will never forget watching the colorful light reflecting off Jack and Joe's faces as Joe counted down the delay between sound and display so that Jack could better predict when the loud noises would happen. At that precise moment, seeing Joe murmuring softly in Jack's ear, I knew there could be no better father for this boy.

When we celebrated Father's Day, I asked each of the kids what they like the most about their dad so we could make him a card. I do this every year; I figure that compiling their words into a homemade card beats standing in line at Victoria's Secret or Home Depot.

And so on Saturday afternoon, while Joe was outside mowing the lawn and the kids were perched at the kitchen island eating lunch, I asked the annual question:

"What's your favorite thing about Dad?"

Henry answered first. "I yike Daddy. Daddy yike cookies. I have a cookie?" No, Henry. No cookies until after lunch.

While his three-year-old brother screeched for a cookie, Joey responded with, "Dad's pretty cool. I mean, he lets me play video games a lot longer than you ever do." Huh. Priorities of a nine-year-old.

(I want a cookie!!)

In between bites of sandwich, four-year-old Rose said dreamily, "Daddy? He's handsome. And you know he's going to marry me. I love him more than I love you." The boys all snickered.

(Coookkiiieeee!)

Six-year-old Charlie, a daddy's boy if ever there was one, had a long list. "I love when he plays baseball with me and when he takes me on the tractor. When he wrestles me at night and we get the mail together. And when he takes me to lunch at TGI Fridays on the last day of school." I reminded him that I was the one who had taken him to lunch. "Oh. I forgot."

Eight-year-old Jack put it succinctly. The conversation went something like this:

Me: "Jack, what do you like most about Dad?"

Jack [robotic voice]: "Really. I like to be with him."

Me: "Anything else, Jack? What do you like to do with Daddy?"

Jack: "To be with him."

Me: "Any special games you like to play?"

Jack [screaming]: "TO. BE. WITH. HIM."

Me [whispering]: "Ssshhhh . . . whisper! This is a surprise!"

Jack: "I don't WHISPER!"

The rest of the conversation quickly disintegrated into something like this:

I want a cookie are you sure you took me to lunch I only remember Dad can I wear your wedding dress when I marry Daddy give me a cookie now can I get the Wii back why do people whisper anyway how about pretzels whispering is dumb I said I was sorry what did we even eat at TGI Fridays?

I started to take some notes about what I would write in Joe's card for the following day. Here's the message I came up with:

Dear Joe,

According to our kids, you are a cookie-eating, tractor-riding, video-game-playing polygamist.

But deep down, we know you're more than that. We know

you're the guy who carries diapers in his gym bag and who launches tickle-fests at bedtime. You're the dad who makes BLTs and sausage when it's your turn to prepare dinner, and you never skimp when squirting whipped cream into a laughing mouth.

Your face lights up whenever you hear Rose's raspy voice.

From family bike rides to making wine, you encourage our family to learn, to grow, to reach higher than we think we can. To help Joey master his multiplication tables, you painstakingly created math charts to review with him nightly, and nothing brings you more pleasure than spending a day in the basement teaching four boys and one girl how to spackle drywall.

You're the one who never saw the autism, just the little blue-eyed boy underneath the diagnosis. And you are tireless in your pursuit to understand that boy as best you can, even if he can't whisper.

We'd like to take a moment on Father's Day to thank you for all the things you do every day, from the dramatic to the ordinary.

And really? We just want to be with you.

A Letter to Henry ❧

EVERY YEAR I WRITE EACH of my children a letter on their birthdays and keep it in a small journal. These letters describe the person they are at that particular age: their likes and dislikes, favorite activities, and overall temperament. This letter is to my youngest son, Henry.

Dear Henry,

We celebrated your third birthday today with a family party at home, and you were delighted with everything from the balloons on the mailbox to your chocolate-frosted cake.

Now a full-fledged toddler, you're still enormous for your age and have caught up to both Rose and Charlie in weight. Your personality is also supersized; from your boisterous laugh to your room-spinning tantrums, you keep us on our toes. You may well be the most stubborn child I've ever met.

Over the summer we took down your crib while you stood by and shouted, "My cwib! I want my cwib!" But within minutes you were thrilled by the prospect of sleeping in the blue car-shaped bed that each of your brothers used when they were toddlers. Now, whenever a guest comes to the house you insist on bringing them upstairs to see your "wace-car bed."

You love things like tomatoes and cheese, but you dislike sweets. Every evening when the rest of the kids scramble for after-dinner treats of popsicles or cookies, you always choose a Greek yogurt. One time we caught you eating it with a serving spoon.

You work hard to keep up with your brothers and sister in everything from the Wii to wrestling, and you always argue for your way. They are incredibly patient with your demands and have affectionately nicknamed you "Twubs," a loving combination of "chubby" and "trouble."

You've picked up on some of Jack's preoccupations, and now we hear you shout, "It's a Toyoya! Mom, a wed Toyoya!" as you identify different cars right alongside your autistic brother.

Sometimes we still refer to you as "the baby," but recently you asked us to call you Batman.

I watch you tumble your way through the world, and I think about how you are the last, the fifth, the final. But you've never really seemed like the youngest; it's as if you were born with the purpose and will of a much older child. You were born knowing what you wanted. And as much as your determination can be trying at times, can make the day seem like one long fight over small moments, I do admire it. I admire the iron strength you so clearly possess, and I know it will serve you well in life.

Every now and again you appear at the side of my bed

in the middle of the night, your blue eyes barely open. In a hushed voice you ask me to "cawwy" you back to your room, and as I stagger down the hallway with your sleepy limbs draped over me, I feel our shared resolve of I-do-it-myself and I-will-give-you-a-timeout of the day soften. I feel our hearts beat together.

And in that slow walk back to your blue race-car bed, I am certain we both understand that you will always be my baby.

Happy Birthday.

Love,

Mom

Lessons at the YMCA ✷

I DESERVE THE MOTHER OF THE YEAR AWARD.

I know that lots of women casually say this, but I mean it. I deserve. The Mother. Of the year. Award.

I recently took all five children for swimming lessons at the Manchester YMCA. Manchester is one of those I-need-to-park-over-there-in-that-parking-garage-across-the-busy-street kind of cities, and as I steered and clutched and directed all five across the double yellow line, I couldn't help but think how the activity I signed up for in the name of summer safety might actually get one of us run over.

At last we arrived at the steps of the Y and burst into the lobby. The lovely young woman behind the reception desk quickly scanned the situation and asked the question I hear whenever I take my spawn out of the basement and into public: "Are they all yours?" I answered with my well-worn joke that I wasn't really sure, but by golly I was going to demand a maternity test one of these days to find out the truth. She smirked and buzzed us in.

We trooped loudly down a long hallway and into the co-ed locker room. I had given the kids instructions earlier in the afternoon, and so they knew that we would use the changing rooms to maintain our privacy from the other people who might be walking through the locker room. With this in mind, Jack leapt up onto a bench and brayed directly into the face of an unsuspecting mother and her two small children.

"You go in THERE to change! So we don't see your PRIVATES! I don't want to see your PRIVATES!"

She barely glanced at me when I tried to explain how his autism sometimes gets in the way of his manners.

Despite the fact that there were three rooms to use, all six of us crammed into one changing room and swapped out clothes for bathing suits, while each boy giggled loudly about my being naked and then took turns threatening to open the door before I had my suit on.

At long last we filed into the pool area and were warmly greeted by our swim instructor, a smiling, wet-haired woman aptly nicknamed "Pools." Pools was an energetic woman with an impressive twenty-year track record of teaching children to swim. She claimed to be unfazed by the afternoon's challenge— showing all five Cariello children how to navigate the shadowy waters of the YMCA pool. She kept her cool even after three-year-old Henry declared her tattoo "scawy." He then added, "I afwaid of you." Meanwhile, my daughter Rose was reassuring everyone around us that I was indeed her mother—and not her grandmother. So much for scoring points with the kind-of-cute lifeguard.

For thirty minutes I alternated between playing "motor-boat" with my forty-five-pound toddler, keeping half an eye on my four-year-old, shooting my older boys dirty looks when they cannonballed on top of Pools, and listening to six-year-old Charlie cry and frantically shriek, "I'm drowning! Help, I'm drowning!"

At the end of our half-hour session, Joey, Jack, and Charlie emerged dripping from the pool. Tearstained, Charlie clutched his floating bubble like it was the last lifeboat on the Titanic. Pools looked shaken. On our way back to the locker room Henry tossed one last insult over his shoulder in her direction. "I no yike you! You face yike a stinky bum!" I whisked him away, explaining that he, too, has autism. (He doesn't. Just bad manners.)

I shuffled them all back to the car in the now-darkened parking garage. On the ride home they alternated between demanding I find LMFAO's "Party Rock" on the radio station and begging me to stop at a taco stand for dinner. Rose requested, in her endearing I-drank-a-case-of-Jack-Daniels-and-it's-time-for-another-cigarette voice, that I use my phone to "text my fadder. To tell him how much I love him."

When we arrived home the kids exploded out of the minivan and into the backyard. I trudged upstairs, weighed down by a bag laden with six wet bathing suits, five soaked towels (Care to guess who had to air dry?) and assorted pairs of underwear left behind by those who chose to ride home commando. I threw it all in the wash so it would be ready for our lesson the following week.

I hoped my award would arrive before then, but somehow I doubted it.

Week Two arrived, and this time I made sure to prepare. I ate well, got a good night's sleep, and even went so far as to take a short afternoon nap with Rose in hopes of looking refreshed and young enough to be her mother rather than her grandmother.

I scored big and found an open parking spot close to the entrance of the Y—and on the same side of the street. I only had to shuffle the kids down two blocks of city sidewalk instead of dragging them all across that double yellow line. Although a shorter walk, Rose still had plenty of time to open and close her winter coat, flashing her tankini at everyone who walked past us. "We're going swimmin'!" she told them in her raspy voice.

Earlier that day I had told Henry he needed to apologize to Pools for calling her face a stinky bum during our first lesson. He giggled and told her, "I sowwy for you. I sowwy I say bad word," as his blue eyes twinkled at the memory. He just couldn't help himself, though, softly muttering "stinky bum" under his breath when she walked away. I let him in the pool anyway. I considered explaining that he really does not have autism — only Jack does — but figured, nah. I should ride this wave as long as I can.

And so the lesson began, complete with motorboat games, illegal cannonballs, and frantic screaming. But half-way through I noticed something miraculous: the three older boys appeared to be swimming. Not flailing, not sinking, but actually using some vaguely recognizable stroke that propelled them from one side of the pool to the other. Pools looked triumphant and rightfully so.

No success ever seems to arrive untarnished, though, and this week the drama shifted from water fun to the vending machines in the Y's lobby. As we walked out of the pool area and down the long hallway towards the machines, each kid planned for the tasty treat they wanted while also negotiating illogical opportunities for sharing. "You can have one of my gummy bears for three pieces of popcorn," and "I'll trade you four pretzels for six M&M's." I frantically checked my wallet for singles; remarkably, I had exactly five one dollar bills. I quickly handed them out, and the kids, just as quickly, fed the machine and made their selections.

I turned around to help Henry open his beloved Doritos just as Jack mistakenly put his dollar in the soda machine. After settling Henry, I told Jack that I didn't have extra change for the soda and that we would need to retrieve his money and put it into the snack machine.

We pushed the button.

Nothing.

Pushed again. Still no money returned.

With a pit in my stomach I turned to my autistic boy and

explained that the machine was broken and that I didn't have any extra dollars to give him. He looked toward the tables, taking in a scene that included each of his siblings happily munching away, and promptly blew a spectrum gasket.

"I hate the Y! I HATE it here! I want a snack! I need a DOLLAR!" He was inconsolable, even as one by one three boys and a girl filed up and offered to share their treat. I decided the best thing to do was leave.

I bustled the kids and their cheese-stained fingers back to the van, and as I closed their door an elderly man stopped me, saying, "God Bless you. Your children are beautiful." He explained how he loves to see big families with a lot of kids.

I peered through the window at all five kids bouncing around the inside of the van. With their usual sibling charms, the other four had worked Jack out of his mood and were taking turns tossing Cheetos into his open mouth.

I guess my award came after all.

And so every Thursday for the next three weeks we trekked back to the Y to meet Pools for lessons. Joey, Jack, and Charlie all made great strides with their swimming. Rose clung to the side of the pool and walked back and forth, proudly declaring she was "swimmin'! For real, Mom, I'm swimmin'!" Henry played on the steps and kept a suspicious eye out for Pools and her "scawwy" tattoo.

By the time our last swimming lesson rolled around I was proud to say I had learned a few things myself. I learned to put my kids in their swimsuits before we left the house, thereby making one less trip to the public changing rooms. I learned the vending machine with soda does not return dollar bills. And I learned you really can teach a Cariello kid to swim. All you need is unending patience and a deaf ear.

This time, as we were leaving the vending area with our orange-stained fingers and soggy t-shirts, I noticed two extremely tall and lean African-American kids enter the lobby. They looked to be high school age, maybe college, and one had a basketball tucked under his arm. As soon as I saw them, a quick uh-oh raced through my mind and my stomach tightened. I tried to corral everyone as I picked up the pace, heading toward the door in an effort to avoid the inevitable.

No luck.

As we passed them Jack bellowed, "That man is really really BLACK!" They both paused for a moment, stunned, then started to laugh awkwardly. I felt my face flush deeply as they walked past me and down the hall. I stammered, trying to explain that Jack has autism.

Jack's loud comment stopped nine-year-old Joey in his tracks. He looked up at me and whispered, "Mom, that isn't right." Looking down at my oldest son's reddened face, I knew I had to try and make it right.

Trying to keep my composure, I called the two boys back. They were clearly uncomfortable; we all were. Once again, I explained that Jack has autism and that it affects his communication. One of them kept saying, "It's okay, don't worry, it's okay" but he wouldn't meet my eyes. I asked them to step over and say hello to Jack, to introduce themselves.

And then, magic.

The two boys bent down. One said, "Hey Jack! How old are you?" while Henry pestered the other boy for his basketball. Jack asked them what grade they were in, and their faces lit up as they explained they were seniors in high school. We learned they come to the YMCA every week to practice together, and they longed to be basketball stars. As they meandered out of the lobby (and held the door for all of us), we learned that they'd grown up two houses away from each other.

We learned they were cousins.

And what did they learn from Jack? I really can't say, but I hope they could look beyond his rude comment and abrupt tone, past his downturned eyes and pointed finger, and see the little boy underneath. I hope they could see what autism sometimes looks like.

Once we were all in the car I started my lecture about keeping our opinions to ourselves, how it's rude to comment on the way someone looks. But I cut it short when the kids started to talk about the cousins. How one was taller than the other, how they wished they could play ball with them. And once again, I learned something: I learned it only took a few minutes in the YMCA lobby to make it right and a few minutes for Jack to learn that people are more than the color of their skin.

Just as he is more than his autism.

That week it wasn't I who deserved the award but two kind basketball players at the YMCA. You're already stars in our eyes.

Although lessons were over, the following week I took the three older boys back to the Y for a chance to practice their swimming. After an hour in the water we decided it was time for a snack and headed to the vending machines once again. As I distributed dollars and instructions, an African-American man walked over to the soda machine and stuck his money in. "Jack!" I hissed in a warning tone, hoping to ward off any comments like the one from the week before.

"WHAT?" he answered at the top of his voice. "I'm not even looking at his skin!"

The People We Meet ❧

IN ADDITION TO THE BEAUTIFUL NETWORK of supportive teachers, family, and friends who have helped us over the years, I've encountered many extraordinary people—many of them accidental strangers—who share their compassion and love for our son Jack. Like shining lampposts along a back road, they often light what might otherwise be a dark path as we travel with our often misunderstood child.

It's the saleswoman who gives me a meaningful look of support when Jack is mid-tantrum over buying gum, and it's the server at Bertucci's who pauses an extra minute and thoughtfully answers Jack's question about her Toyota Prius. It's the developmental specialist who thinks of him as "Jack" rather than as "Child," and it's the preschool teacher who takes Jack under her wing and slowly, slowly coaxes him into speaking sentences one single word at a time.

These are people who see not only what Jack has but

who he is. They take the time to glimpse the little boy hiding behind his preoccupations with cars and birthdays, radios and dogs, and can see a child struggling to connect socially despite his disability. They don't set out to change our lives, yet still they effect small changes to my heart with little—usually unintended—acts of kindness. We've encountered many, many of these special people over the years, but whenever anybody asks me about the people Jack meets, three in particular are always the first to come to mind.

About a year ago we did a major renovation to the entire downstairs of our house. The noise, disruption, and chaos sent Jack into a tailspin, and every day after school I had to coax him just to walk up the driveway and into the house. Matt, our general contractor, became a permanent fixture, one of the few recurring faces amongst the endless stream of construction people who flowed in and out of the door each day. Childless himself, this tough, burly man connected well with all of our kids and worked hard to ease Jack's tension as each new phase of the project unfolded. He would tell him things like "Jack, tomorrow we're going to start installing the floors. It's gonna be loud!"

The only problem was Maggie, Matt's beloved yellow lab. Most days Maggie traveled shotgun in Matt's red pickup truck, her head lolling in the wind, and while the other kids loved it, Jack was beside himself. Although he's afraid of most animals, Jack's especially fearful of dogs. For reasons we don't quite understand, he's been terrified of them since he was about two, and being within a mile of one can set him off. We've asked many times what he's so afraid of, but with Jack's limited communication skills the best he's ever offered us is "Dogs are scary. They should live in cages." My suspicion is that their unpredictable and quick movements make him anxious. He has a hard enough time figuring out people's facial expressions, and he seems totally confused about animals. With dogs, he often shouts things like "He will bite me! That dog is MAD!"

Every day I steeled myself for an outburst as Jack walked past the truck with a wary look on his face, as if he were afraid that Maggie herself might somehow use her large paws to open the door handle and spring out at him. And every day I vowed I would talk to Matt and insist he leave Maggie at home, that it was too much for Jack, that we were already asking a lot of him by gutting his favorite bathroom. (He peed in the woods a lot that summer.)

But each day the walk past the red pickup truck got a little easier. Matt, a man who is given more to observation than interaction, quietly watched Jack's progress and started taking baby steps to introduce boy and dog. Nearly every day for all of August, Matt would slowly ease Maggie out of the truck and call to Jack, asking if he wouldn't like to feel how soft her fur was or throw her a tennis ball.

Truly, I thought he was crazy. We could hardly get Jack to watch a dog do tricks on *America's Funniest Home Videos*, never mind tolerate one in his own driveway. And although Jack never quite managed to touch Maggie, every day this gentle man made it his mission to make our son just a little bit more comfortable, a little bit less scared. He—and his equally gentle companion—gave us hope that one day Jack might overcome his deeply-rooted dog phobia.

And then there was Texas Mike, the painter who worked on our front porch last fall. (We bought a fixer-upper, okay?) Weighing probably no more than a hundred pounds and with dreadlocks down to his bony hips, Texas Mike was an authentic cowboy who spoke mostly in monosyllables. On the first day he showed up at our house with a battered radio in hand, and immediately Jack wanted to know every last detail not only about that radio but about every radio Texas Mike had ever owned, along with information about his music selection, why he drove a Subaru Legacy, and his mother. How old was she? Jack wanted to know. Had she died yet?

Every time I looked outside, Jack was trailing close enough behind Texas Mike to pull on a dreadlock, all the while firing questions at him like a human machine gun. I never really heard Mike respond with more than one-word sentences, and I figured his patience was wearing thin.

I tried to explain that Jack had autism, and that was why he fixates on unusual subjects like radios and birthdays. Until my own dying breath I'll never forget the way Texas Mike slowly gazed down at Jack, then slowly back to me, and in a drawn-out Texas drawl softly voiced the four most beautiful words I'd ever heard:

"Looks al-raht to me."

Why yes, Texas Mike, he looks alright to me, too. Thank you for reminding me that he really *is* alright.

This spring, not long after our renovations were finished, Jack developed a crush on our teenage neighbor, Kristin. Ever the Prince Charming, he showed his deep love by marching up to her and drilling her with questions about what kind of phone she had, how many languages she knew, and what kind of music she liked. Throughout the entire month of April, Jack spent every afternoon perched on our front steps watching for her bus. As soon as it arrived and the doors flew open he would shout down to the street something like "Kristin! It's Jack! I just downloaded Michael Jackson from iTunes!"

Thankfully, Kristin isn't the typical teenage girl who gets embarrassed when a second-grade boy meets her at the bus braying the lyrics to "Thriller." She isn't the sort of teenager who hates being made a spectacle of or is uncomfortable around people with social disabilities. She took Jack's admiration in stride and went out of her way to make him feel special.

Although extremely kind all the time, Kristin really demonstrated her thoughtfulness when, on Jack's seventh birthday, she met him at the bus stop with a card she'd made. (Apparently homemade cards are popular in my neighborhood. Perhaps I started a trend with the whole Father's Day thing.) There was Kristin, getting up much earlier than usual to make sure she caught Jack in time, and there was the homemade card, and there was Jack with immeasurable joy on his face. The combination was extraordinary.

Each of these people touched me in very different ways. Matt taught me that with the right amount of patience and perseverance we can help Jack tackle even his biggest phobias. Texas Mike reminded me to relax, take a deep Texan breath, and enjoy this little boy for exactly who he is. And Kristin showed me that Jack resides as firmly in other people's hearts as he does in mine.

Sometimes it takes another set of eyes to see what I can't, but I know one thing for sure: with people like this in our lives, it really is *al-raht.*

Dogs on Parade ❧

FOR AS LONG AS I CAN REMEMBER, Jack's been terrified of animals.

My most vivid memory of his animal phobia is from the summer of 2008 when we took the whole family to the Fourth of July parade in a neighboring town. My husband Joe has a weakness for patriotic events, and he's especially fond of parades, so every year we get all decked out in our matching red, white, and blue, and the seven of us troop into Amherst, New Hampshire, to enjoy the festivities in the center of town. (Translation: Joe stands ahead of us and waves to patients and fellow townspeople like the Mayor of Whoville, while I maneuver the behemoth double stroller through the crowd and hand out cotton candy to five overheated, cranky children. Thankfully July 4th comes but once a year.)

Our first parade was especially memorable, but for all the wrong reasons. Fresh from the fireworks display the night before, four-year-old Jack was outraged at the idea of attending another noisy, overcrowded event. (And frankly, so was I.) We created a social story to explain the event, and we jollied him along with the promise of an ice cream cone and a quiet afternoon at home.

Arriving about half an hour before the parade started, we parked our blankets at the curb and introduced ourselves to the families with young children flanking us on both sides. Jack was acting a little erratic, and at one point I explained to the family on my right how he's on the autism spectrum and that both crowds and animals made him anxious and fearful. Especially dogs.

He started to really unravel when a man wearing a cowboy hat loped by and tied his horse to a tree about thirty feet behind us. Jack kept asking if horses bite and he insisted that I hold him so he could keep a watchful eye over my shoulder. Distracted by the horse, he was facing the wrong way when the parade started. As we caught sight of the procession in the distance I heard our brand-new friends to the right of us say, "Oh . . . this isn't going to be good," predicting Jack's reaction to the annual starting tradition: the Dog Parade.

People in town are encouraged to bring their four-legged friends and march with them on a leash. I'm talking well over a hundred dogs here, big and small. Great danes, beagles, shepherds, and bulldogs. Poodles, goldens, shelties, and mutts. You name it and it's likely in the Amherst Fourth of July Parade. They trotted past, some dressed in finery, and as soon as Jack caught sight of them he let out an ear-piercing wail and buried his head in my shoulder until they were gone.

Next we were assaulted by a battalion of massive horse-drawn carriages filled with men dressed like Paul Revere. You could just barely hear Jack's screams over the thundering hooves and shooting cannons. As they rounded the corner and out of sight, Joe and I looked at each other and breathed a sigh of relief, but then Charlie hollered out, "Look! A monkey!" Good grief! I thought. What kind of parade is this? Did we take a wrong turn and land in the circus? Stricken, Jack looked at me with his tear-stained face and mouthed, "Monkey?" Luckily, the monkey was just a clown's hand puppet. Jack slumped against me, exhausted by the ordeal.

He demanded two ice cream cones that afternoon, and we figured he deserved at least that many. (I had two myself.)

His phobia is incapacitating, and it affects all of us. If we're invited to someone's house for dinner and they have a dog, I have to call ahead and diplomatically ask if the family pet can be kept in another room during our visit. When we're all together in the car, the kids will start shouting, "Look out my side, Jack! Don't look out the other window!" just to distract him from noticing a dog walking with its owner down the street. We all feel the stress from his strong reactions. Two years earlier, when Joe managed to coax him through that zoo in Maine, we thought that perhaps his fear might be subsiding. But he still won't go near an animal that isn't caged or restricted in some way.

Last summer we enjoyed a beautiful day at the beach.

Although Jack spent a fair amount of time shouting things like "I hate you!" at the sea gulls flying overhead, he still managed to have some fun in the water. After a full afternoon we packed all of our stuff up, and on the long walk back to the car we encountered an older man walking a giant German Shepherd. As he started to cross the street toward us Jack started to flap his hands and whimper. Weighed down by a chubby toddler, countless bags overflowing with wet towels, and a large umbrella, Joe and I struggled to quickly contain the scene and to keep the other kids calm. All at once, something primal came over me, and I barked out, "Sir! You must take your dog a different way! He's freaking out!" The man asked "Who? Who is freaking out?" with a confused look on his face. "My son!" I shot back, thinking, What the hell is the matter with him? Can't he see Jack's losing control? Then suddenly the picture snapped into focus, and I saw specific details very clearly: the man's blurry eyes and baffled expression, the dog's bright orange collar.

A blind man and his service dog.

Not exactly my finest hour. Even Joe was embarrassed by my outburst and gave me a long hug by the car.

Then suddenly, this past winter, progress.

Every year over winter break we take the kids to an indoor water park about two hours north of here for a couple of days. They anticipate this trip all year, and each time we do it the same way, spending the afternoon playing at Kahuna Laguna, followed by dinner at the Moosehead Restaurant, and a night at the Hampton Inn. (The first year Jack wouldn't get out of the car at the restaurant because he was afraid there was a real moose inside.) This year we followed the same routine and arrived at the hotel around eight in the evening, exhausted after a full day of water slides and wading pools, and then dinner.

Joe dropped me off in the lobby with the five kids and went back to the car for the rest of the bags. As soon as we walked in Joey tugged my hand and said, "Mom, get Jack. There's a dog in here." Sure enough, I looked over and saw a midsized, light brown dog standing with his owners across from the reception desk.

Jack caught sight of the dog at about the same time as I did, and he immediately channeled his anxiety into bossy mode and went barreling up to the desk, actually bowling people out of the way to get to the manager. With his pointer finger raised high above his head, he indignantly brayed in her face, "HELLO-O! There's a DOG in here! Dogs are NOT ALLOWED in HOTELS!" Taken aback, she explained how this particular Hampton Inn was now pet-friendly. He huffed away and started orbiting the room, making sure to give the dog a wide berth.

Joe came in laden with bags a moment later and within a nanosecond took in the scene: Jack swirling around the room muttering to himself, the kids and I scattered, and the dog in the center, twitching her slender tail. I caught Joe's eye and gave him a signal to wait, to hold back and see what happened. Jack's remaining in the lobby was itself a milestone, and I was curious to see my son's next move. I gestured for the other kids to relax and let him be, and then I made my way over to the dog's owners to explain why Jack was so distressed.

What happened next was breathtaking.

The man with the dog, named Gracie, sat down next to his pet and in the midst of the noise and movement, began to calmly call out to Jack.

"Jack. I'm waiting for you. I'm waiting for you to pet my dog."

Jack looked over in surprise, and the man said again, "Jack. I'm here, and Gracie and I are waiting."

Still circling the room, Jack began to loop ever closer and closer each time until he was just a few feet from Gracie. The man continued his gentle requests, asking that Jack touch Gracie, that they were waiting for him. I held my breath as Jack tentatively reached out his hand to pet, first, the man's hair, and then extended his fingers to graze Gracie's short, tan coat.

"She's soft!" he exclaimed and bounced away. In tears, I turned to the family and tried to convey what a miracle this moment was.

I'll never fully understand what exactly convinced Jack to let his guard down and finally approach Gracie.

The next morning at breakfast we ran into the same family again, and Jack asked where Gracie was and where she had slept. We chatted for a while, and they explained that Gracie was a rescue from Turks & Caicos, an area apparently overrun with strays. When we got home I went online, curious to read about this kind of dog, and I learned that Gracie is considered a potcake, a mixed breed named for the scraps of food they're given from the bottom of the rice pot.

Shortly after our success with Gracie the Potcake, we decided to be a little more proactive and talked to our psychologist about methods we could use to further Jack's progress with animals. She suggested conducting a kind of "dog therapy," where we would visit a home with a calm dog and give Jack as much time and space as he needed to become comfortable. Joe's sister had adopted a year-old lab-mix, and everyone in the family said he was remarkably easygoing: a perfect dog to introduce to Jack.

As with the zoo trip, Jack appeared unfazed when we announced at breakfast the day before that we were going to visit Aunt Ann Marie so we could meet her dog. He continued shoveling his Honey-Nut Cheerios in his mouth at a breakneck pace but managed, in between large spoonfuls, to ask about the dog's name. I showed him pictures of his cousins lying and sleeping with the dog, Charra, and I used a social story to explain how the visit would unfold. Throughout the day I waited for his anxiety to surface, and I kept close watch on him during the hour-long car ride to her house the next day. Nothing. But when we pulled up Jack said nervously, "I'm not sure I want to meet that dog." We encouraged him to walk up the steps and into the foyer with us, where Aunt Ann Marie and Uncle Jim were waiting with Charra.

Within seconds Jack hit his red zone, shrieking and

covering his ears. Two other small Cariello children followed his lead and started screaming and jumping around whenever the poor animal moved. Jack climbed on top of (very tall) Uncle Jim and begged, "Carry me on your shoulders for the day!" In an attempt to put a lid on the already bubbling pot of chaos, Joe kept telling Jack to stop screaming, to calm down, that the loud noise was upsetting the dog. Charra, misinterpreting the kids' excitement for play, jumped up and started barking, accidentally nipping three-year-old Henry in the nose. Incensed, Henry shouted, "That dog bite me! He bite me in the FACE! I no yike him!"

Jack—and Henry—spent the next hour perched on barstools in the kitchen, each keeping a baleful eye out for the dog and listening for the jangle of his collar. We reminded Jack to use his deep, calming breaths but to no avail. He remained jumpy and nervous, finally retreating to the basement, a safe place because Charra doesn't like the carpeted stairs. When we announced that it was time to go, Jack raced up from the basement, called out, "Bye Aunt Ann Marie!" and slammed the door behind him.

Not quite the breakthrough we were hoping for.

But, as with all of Jack's journeys, there are always small moments of progress guiding us toward our larger goals, and the biggest breakthrough of the day came later when I put him to bed. As I leaned over to kiss his soft cheek goodnight, Jack whispered softly, "I tried with that dog. But I screamed because I was scared."

Maybe we didn't have much success converting Jack into

a dog lover, but he did make a remarkable leap in communication that day. He'd never been able to explain his behavior or feelings about an animal before.

Baby steps.

A couple of weeks later Jack presented me with a picture he'd made of our family. Each person was drawn in a different color — Rose was a little hard to see since her silhouette was entirely in yellow — and floating near our shoulders was an image of a dog and a cat. I reminded Jack that we didn't have a dog or a cat.

"No, we don't," he agreed.

I told him how much I liked his picture, then tentatively asked him what their names were. I was curious to see if he was at last opening up to the idea of our family having pets.

"The cat is named Toilet, and the dog is named Underwear," he giggled into the palm of his hand.

Yep. Definitely getting closer.

A Letter to Joey ❧

Dear Joey,

You've just celebrated your ninth birthday, and it's been another wonderful year. We've watched you blossom into an avid reader (the Harry Potter series), a somewhat interested baseball player (less dandelion-picking than last year), and a Lego fanatic (you just finished Hagrid's Hut).

You continue to handle your role as eldest of our clan with grace and ease. Each of your siblings, especially six-year-old Charlie, competes for your attention, and it's sweet to see you direct them during play time. It's especially endearing to watch you with three-year-old Henry. Although you crave quiet space amongst the madness, I see you work hard to maintain your composure when your patience is tested (like that time Henry smashed Hagrid's Hut into pieces with Rose's mini saucepan).

You and Jack have a very interesting relationship, and I've

really enjoyed watching it grow and change. As you learned this year, Jack has autism, and it can make things somewhat challenging for you.

We waited to tell you about Jack's diagnosis simply because we didn't think it was information you needed or were ready to process. But I think you always knew he was different. One time in the kitchen we were all enjoying a family favorite—breakfast for dinner—and you and Charlie were fooling around like the crazy boys you are. Ten minutes into it I lost my patience and threatened to separate the two of you. You protested, arguing that Charlie was your "best brother." Gritting my teeth, I asked about Jack. Wasn't he a "best brother," too? You calmly replied, "No Mom, Jack isn't normal." What followed wasn't pretty: the mama bear in me started bellowing things like "Why isn't he normal? Why?" Ever the cool cucumber, you nodded your head toward the other end of the table where Jack sat, nonchalantly blowing his nose into his pancake. He then rolled the whole thing up and popped it into his mouth.

Okay. Maybe not so normal.

Then one day it was official. You came home from Lego club and asked, "Does Jack have autism?" You went on to ask questions I'd been hiding in my heart for years. Would he always be autistic? Would he ever get married? Is that why he hates dogs?

A few summers ago we accepted a much-anticipated invitation to your friend Josh's birthday party, where there would be a giant water slide. As the time for the party drew near, you became alarmed when you saw me packing Jack's bathing suit.

"Please, Mom, can't he stay home?" you pleaded. I explained that the invitation said it was okay to bring siblings, and Jack loves parties. (Plus, Daddy was looking forward to taking a nap with the babies that afternoon.) You complained, saying, "You'll start talking to the other moms, and you won't watch him, Mom. You won't!" (Note for future, young lad: I might have relented if you hadn't challenged my parenting. I dug my heels in.) Of course I would watch him! I'm his mother!

Fast-forward to later that afternoon when I was relaxing distractedly with some of the other parents. I looked up just in time to see Jack scale the large water slide—sans bathing suit. Your angry glare was not lost on me.

I asked you once if you ever felt embarrassed by Jack at school, and I braced myself for your answer. Would it be the time he held up the entire bus, kicking and screaming because he didn't feel like getting on? Or maybe the day he whirled like a tornado through the school-wide book fair? Perhaps it would be Jack's latest habit of asking everyone what color their shampoo is. You thought for a minute and said that, yes, sometimes you were a little embarrassed by something he does. As the pit in my stomach grew you casually explained that you wished he wouldn't give you such a huge hug and kiss whenever you passed each other in the hall because it made your friends laugh.

I know it can't be easy being Jack's brother. It can't be easy having a sibling who has a breakdown at the mere sight of a four-legged animal or greets you at the end of the driveway after school dressed only in his underwear while bellowing the lyrics to Michael Jackson's "Man in the Mirror." Although I know you suffer to some degree because one of your siblings has autism, I'm confident there is a positive side to our family's dynamic for both of you.

For starters, I don't feel sorry for you because you have a brother with autism. Jack brings a richness to your life that all those so-called normal families miss out on, and you are learning as much from him as he is from you. Because of Jack, you are learning how to anticipate others' needs before your own, like warning us when a dog is approaching the bus stop. And you're learning how to communicate more creatively. For the longest time you would communicate to Jack through me, but now we're at the point where you know how to elicit answers from him. ("Jack, look at me. Look in my eyes. Now where did you hide my gum?")

Nothing gives your father and me more pleasure than to hear the two of you converse, play a game, or make mischief together. Last week Jack asked me what he should do if "my friends are mean to me" and referred to some kind of game they played with him at lunch time. Without any cue from me, you hopped off your stool, went over to him and explained just what type of game the kids were playing in the cafeteria and how he could avoid their taunting.

Just this afternoon we were preparing to head out and see *Kung Fu Panda 2* when Jack suddenly refused to go. I was surprised—Jack loves movies—but you explained that he doesn't like the main character, Po, because he's scary. I turned and asked him if this was true, and he said, "Yes, Po scares me. I'm staying home." Sometimes you understand him better than I do.

Jack benefits from you. Without even knowing it, you push him to be a better version of himself all the time. By your example, he works harder to communicate effectively and to achieve the goals he's seen you accomplish. I don't think we can all fully understand the importance a boy barely a year older plays in Jack's development, but I'm certain it's nothing but positive. The evidence is the love in his eyes and those big embarrassing bear hugs at school.

I wonder if one day you're going to look back on your childhood with Jack and feel bitter, like you were short-changed in some way. I doubt it. I think you'll appreciate the value of Jack's brotherhood as the two of you continue to grow your relationship and mature together. He may not be "normal," and he may like a certain flavor of pancake, but he's making each one of us a better person in his own way. On behalf of Jack, I'd like to thank you for being such an extraordinary brother.

I know if Jack could, he'd thank you himself.

Happy Birthday, my dear son.

Love,

Mom

What Does Heaven Look Like? ❧

BOTH JOE AND I WERE RAISED AS CATHOLICS, and we made a commitment to continue the faith with our children. We had each baptized when they were infants, and our oldest boys attend weekly classes in religious education. Joey and Jack have made their First Communion.

Admittedly, Joe has a greater dedication to Catholicism than I do. Except for my driving them to their classes on Tuesday afternoons, he guides the religious ship in the Cariello household. Every Sunday he organizes three, sometimes four, disgruntled children and gets them to church in time for ten-thirty Mass. Despite a lot of protests and under-the-breath comments like "Can't we ever skip church?" he marches them out the door towards redemption and rewards good behavior with a doughnut afterward. I rarely go.

Joe reminds us of the greater meaning behind holidays like Christmas and Easter, and is always prepared with a bit of religious history. He leads prayers at mealtimes and talks about things like the "message from the gospel today" when he gets back from church on Sundays. He pores over the weekly church bulletin, catching up on community news and upcoming church-y events.

I personally have no issue with Catholicism, and I consider my relationship with God to be strong and spiritual. I enjoy church when I do go: the quiet time for reflection, the meaningful start to a family Sunday, revisiting the traditions of my childhood. So why don't I go more often, you ask? Why don't I unite with Joe and attend regularly with my family? Well, I'm a bit ashamed of my answer, but here it is: I go to yoga instead. My Bikram Yoga studio holds an eight o'clock class on Sunday mornings, which I faithfully attend every week before racing home just before Joe heads out, leaving me behind with three-year-old Henry (who belongs in church even less than I do).

As with many things in my life, Jack has helped me see religion from a different angle, especially since nonliteral concepts like God and heaven are hard for him to wrap his head around. He's been attending church regularly since he was about five, and at around age six he started asking a lot of questions, like:

—When do you think you're going to die?

—What does heaven look like?

—Why did God make us butt cracks?

—Did God decide traffic rules?

—What is God's last name?

—Do you eat in heaven?

—Will I be born to the same mother after heaven or a different family?

We've done our very best to answer these questions as accurately as we know how, which mostly means telling him things like "I don't know" or "Wow! That's a great question, Jack!"

And really, he asks good questions. We simply don't have answers to all of them. (Except for the one about traffic rules. That one was pretty easy.) Instead we've tried to flex Jack's mind by asking him what he thinks heaven looks like and whether he thinks someone would need to eat or sleep there. I even asked him if he'd like to be born to the same mother again or to someone different, then I held my breath, worried he'd suggest a game change. He eyed me suspiciously and said, "You again. I guess."

(We've never really addressed the one about butt cracks. I pretended I hadn't heard him.)

The interesting thing is, Jack seems to enjoy the Catholic rituals. He accepts church as just another Sunday activity and does the least amount of complaining when it's time to go. And much to his brother Joey's chagrin, Jack doesn't limit mealtime prayers to our table at home. He's been known to bray out, "In the name of the FATHER, SON, and

HOLY SPIRIT!" before he digs into his corn dog and fries at a restaurant. Meanwhile, the other kids bury their heads in embarrassment.

"What? Say your PRAYER before you EAT!"

Even though I don't attend church regularly, I do love watching my children perform the traditional Catholic sacraments. I was greatly moved at each of their baptisms and delighted when Joey made his First Communion. Dressing them in special clothing for the occasion and partaking of these rituals is very special to me, and we always plan elaborate celebrations afterwards.

Except for an unfortunate swearing incident (where he let out a string of curse words when the teacher unexpectedly turned the lights out to show a movie), Jack was fairly successful in completing his religion classes. For one hour a week he gamely listened to stories about the apostles and made crafts, like a Noah's Ark, out of popsicle sticks. His teacher reported that he usually sat quietly in the back.

As first grade ends, the students are required to stand before the director of religious education, Mrs. Danielson, and recite their prayers before they can advance to second grade. This sounds a lot more intimidating than it really is; Mrs. Danielson is a lovely woman and spends a fair amount of time helping the kids relax before asking to hear their prayers. Joey breezed through it, and given Jack's astounding memory, I had no doubt he'd do fine, too.

For weeks we worked on a prayer each evening, and by the appointed date I felt like Jack was ready. We headed over to the church on a rainy April afternoon, and Mrs. Danielson welcomed us into her homey office. As she showed Jack pictures of her own son and shared stories of her childhood, Jack became increasingly antsy. Nervous myself, I suggested that maybe he could chew some gum to help him calm down. He agreed, and in between bites of Trident Jack started his prayers. Every now and again Mrs. Danielson would prompt him when he stalled, and it was smooth sailing until we came to the last one, the Act of Contrition.

Jack stopped about halfway through, and it seemed as though he'd run out of gas. He started to jump around and stim, sure signs that he'd had enough. I started to gather up our things to leave—he was tired and he does have autism, after all. I figured he'd satisfied the requirements well enough, but no. . . . Mrs. Danielson recommended I take him out to the waiting room to collect himself and then return when he was ready to finish.

Back in the waiting room Jack became increasingly agitated. I had him do some wall push-ups and jumping jacks to help him regulate and told him that as soon as he finished this last prayer, we could go. After about ten minutes of whining (Jack), negotiating (Jack), and outright pleading (me), he agreed to return to the office and plunked himself back into the chair with a loud sigh.

"Are you ready, Jack?" Mrs. Danielson asked kindly. "Let's start from the beginning."

"NO!" he barked back at her. "I'll start where I left off."

And sure enough, he picked up the line exactly where

he'd ended before the break and finished reciting the Act of Contrition without a hitch and on his terms. We went to Friendly's to celebrate.

Having successfully negotiated Mrs. Danielson, Jack moved ahead to the second grade and in the fall began preparing for his First Communion. I was excited for Jack's big day, excited to see him in a new suit, excited to watch him walk down the aisle with his class, and excited to celebrate afterwards. It was going to be great.

My image of Jack's perfect First Communion started to fray around the edges about a week before the event, when I took him to the rehearsal in the church. Something set him off on the way there, and he decided he wasn't going. During the ten-minute drive he whined and flapped his hands, twisting around in his seat and begging to go home.

So I all but dragged him in, whispering things in his ear like "You will do this!" and "Please get through this, and I will buy you a doughnut!" Meanwhile he screamed things like "I hate church!" and, inexplicably, "I want to dye my hair red!" He said he was blind and walked in with his arms outstretched and his eyes closed, claiming "I can't see anyone! They're not here! It's canceled!" Then he hid under the piano.

During the entire week between the rehearsal and the actual ceremony, I continually quelled a rising panic whenever I thought about how he would perform come Saturday. I spoke several times with Mrs. Danielson, and we created contingency plans in the event that Jack wouldn't walk down the aisle with his class, wouldn't sit still during the Homily, or wouldn't receive communion.

In short, if by Saturday he still had autism.

Complicating the matter was Jack's tendency to be extremely literal. In religious education class the teacher had explained how, during First Communion, the host would transform from an ordinary wafer into Jesus himself. During the rehearsal, the children were counseled that Jesus would be in their mouths and bodies, and that they should treat him respectfully.

Literal boys like Jack, boys who start looking around wildly for giraffes when their mother announces that the Walmart parking lot is a zoo, do not warm up to the idea of Jesus in their mouths.

Saturday morning he gamely put his new suit on and walked proudly to the car. He sat with his class during the half-hour before the ceremony and even participated in the group picture. When it was time to line up, he stood in place and waited for the kids ahead of him to shuffle up the stairs. As I held my breath, he began the slow walk down the aisle with his partner and turned into his assigned pew just as Mass began.

Success.

Mrs. Danielson and I exchanged hopeful glances, and I nearly burst into tears from the emotional pressure. Joe and I were stationed right behind Jack so we could poke, prod, and if necessary remove him should the self-stimulation in his body take over and he could no longer remain still. We sat at attention, nervous and watchful.

And then Jack did what he so often does when we least expect it; he gave the stressful morning a little sparkle. About two-thirds of the way through the ceremony, the choir began to sing "Lamb of God." Jack turned over his shoulder to us, his face beaming, and loudly announced, "This is my very favorite song of the whole day!" He turned back around in his seat and sang the verses at the top of his voice, with his hands rising and falling as the melody, and my heart, swelled.

Amidst all the formality and ceremony, all the tradition and fanfare, God left a little room for Jack's very favorite song of the whole day.

Mistakes were made, of course. On his way to receive communion, instead of placing his left hand over his right the way we practiced, practiced, practiced, Jack simply held out his left hand like he was expecting the priest to make change for a dollar bill. Walking toward the pew he threw his head back and tossed in the host the way you might throw back a handful of peanuts. And unbeknownst to us, he wore gym socks with his new shoes.

After he had returned to the pew, Mass continued and the invisible ants of self-stimulation slowly crawled up Jack's body; his rocking increased but fortunately not to the point where he needed to get up and leave the church.

At the end of the ceremony, Joe and I met up with Jack down in the church basement where all of the children were waiting. As we walked up the darkened stairs and into the bright sunlight of the May morning, Jack seemed to glow from within with pride. He was as calm, as sure of himself, as I'd ever seen him. Back at the house he serenely accepted praise and gifts from all of our guests, a quiet smile playing on his lips.

A few weeks after Jack's First Communion, Joe returned from church and recited a portion of Psalm 118, the message from that morning's gospel. We both agreed it perfectly captured Jack's experiences in church, in our family, and with his autism.

"The stone that the builders rejected has now become the cornerstone."

Bless you, my little lamb Jack. You are, in so many ways, our cornerstone.

Obsession ·●

LIKE MOST KIDDOS ON THE SPECTRUM, Jack often becomes preoccupied with random things, fixating for a while and then suddenly losing interest in favor of something else.

Okay, maybe preoccupied isn't the right term. He becomes obsessed.

Jack's tendency to fixate started very early, long before he had been diagnosed. At only ten months old he became infatuated with a particular *Baby Einstein* movie called "Baby Bach." More than a dozen times in a single morning he would crawl over to the entertainment center, fish the DVD case out of a stack of many, and attempt to stuff it into the television himself. For months it was the only thing that soothed him; he would sit in front of the TV and rock to the songs over and over and over. (This is a chilling memory for me.)

Somewhere around the age of three he started setting the table for some kind of imaginary meal. All day long he would rummage around in the lower cabinets and silverware drawer for cups and plates and spoons, then would set the table to match the exact number of people in the house at that moment. If someone came or went he would scurry over and rearrange the settings to reflect the change. He spent an entire Thanksgiving lining up forks and mugs in some peculiar order that only he understood. (Again, chilling.)

As time passed and he acquired speech, he moved on to preoccupations where he actually engaged with other people. At age five he started asking everyone the color of their shampoo. We were relieved that he was at last attempting to make conversation, and he experienced such obvious joy when given this odd information that it was hard not to share in his enthusiasm.

"Purple!" he'd chortle, a giant grin spreading across his face. "My teacher's shampoo is *purple*."

He stored shampoo facts for teachers and neighbors and family, and he always tagged it onto the end of someone's name. "Miss Nancy? Her shampoo is green."

This went on and on and on for months, and then, just as quickly as the obsession had formed, he dropped it altogether and latched on to birthdays instead. For the next couple of months he questioned everyone about when they were born. He stored hundreds of birthdays for families, friends, and neighbors. Jack astounded the woman who lives across the street one day when he waved to her from the driveway and robotically shouted, "Your birthday is September 20th!"

The summer after he turned six Jack developed his fascination with cars and trucks, and like all of his fixations, collecting this data started out as a cute preoccupation. But within days it exploded into a full-fledged obsession. Instead of asking when someone's birthday was, he would point his finger in their face and bark, "What kind of car do you drive?" Being in the car with Jack that summer was like riding with a member of the census bureau. Based on his observations, Hondas and Toyotas are among the most popular vehicles in New Hampshire, with Acuras a distant third. When I started to consider not only the brands but all of the *models* of cars, I figured this particular fixation could keep Jack busy for decades. And our earnest, literal Jack, for whom memorizing the make, model, shape, size, color, and fuel source wasn't enough, also wanted to know what each car name meant. Have you ever considered what "Prius" means? Or how to explain the term "Legacy" to a six-year-old?

Responses to his question varied, but it often made people uncomfortable to have a child glare at them and demand to know the make and model of their vehicle. Since social cues are difficult for Jack to decipher, he didn't notice how his unblinking stare and pointing finger made his unsuspecting victims somewhat anxious. He wanted answers, and he went to great lengths to get them. Many people squirmed. Some snickered and looked away while they pretended they didn't hear him. Others made up cute names: "Why, my car? Oh, I call my car Shadow! Because it's *black*!"

If I thought the questioning was getting out of hand I would step in to redirect Jack, often mouthing "autism" as I ruffled his soft, brown crew cut with my fingers. But sometimes I sat back and watched them stammer. It was like being an observer on the sidelines as a bizarre social experiment unfolded. Most curious to me were the people who just couldn't (or wouldn't) divulge this information. It baffled me every time. It's a car, and he's six. If you're reluctant to admit you're driving a top-of-the-line Mercedes, than make something up. Pretend you drive a dented, grey Toyota Sienna littered with goldfish crackers. Anything so we can all get on with our lives.

It was all very revealing, this car business. How did our college-age server at Olive Garden end up driving a Lexus? ("My mother's car," she mumbled with a self-conscious shrug.) Or how about the CEO of a major company tooling around in a Dodge Neon? Cars seemed to say a lot about their drivers, and each bit of data that Jack gathered seemed to have a story behind it just waiting to be filled in.

However, the person most revealed by the car obsession was Jack himself. Through this newest fixation he gave us another subtle peek into his fascinating brain. That can be the beauty of autism—it gives all of us a rare glimpse inside an intricate, complicated mind.

As a parent, I occasionally revel in the awe of others as Jack recites the information he has somehow stored. Why, maybe he is a genius! Maybe memorizing every Volvo,

Nissan, and Cadillac will have a big payoff for Jack one day! Maybe he'll be the Temple Grandin of the auto industry and they'll make a movie about his life that will win an Oscar or an Emmy and then he'll stand up and ask the cameras to point to his loving, caring mother and I'll be wearing a couture gown that was designed just for me and hides the fact that I've birthed five children.

Believe it or not, an even better scenario unfolded.

About halfway through the summer we realized that Jack wasn't simply collecting information to categorize and store in his mind alongside all those bizarre stats about shampoo and birthdays. Instead, these obsessions provided him with the chance to interact with people — often strangers — about a subject he likes. "What kind of car do you drive?" is the "Hello. How are you? My name is Jack" of his world. It bridges a social gap that might otherwise seem as wide to him as the English Channel.

It's beautiful watching our socially limited son create ways to make himself comfortable talking to people. Even more beautiful is watching as he gradually learns to turn their answers into a conversation. "Oh! A Toyota! I like Toyotas! What color is yours?" More than once that summer I had to look away while my eyes filled with tears and my heart leaped with joy. Behavior we thought of as sometimes annoying, occasionally funny, and always peculiar was something else entirely.

It was progress.

As is so often the case with Jack and his autism, there's a learning curve for us as much as for him. We can't always take his quirkiness at face value—we have to look inside, around, and beyond his mysterious behavior to see what drives it.

(Pun intended.)

Karate ❧

WHEN JACK WAS FOUR we enrolled him in a karate class. Our intentions were two-fold: we thought that it would be good to have him burn off some of his endless energy, and we also hoped that he would benefit from the socialization of being with a group of kids all participating in the same sport.

It was an unmitigated disaster.

Every Saturday morning we dressed him in his stiff, white uniform, and Joe drove him to the local karate studio near where we were living in Bedford. For almost the entire class Jack would whirl and spin around the room's circumference, circling and circling while the instructor worked the rest of the students through choreographed movements and talked about things like *discipline* and *respect*. Joe spent the majority of the hour chasing our son around the studio, trying to get him to mimic the exercises.

Jack just didn't get it. He didn't get that you weren't

supposed to take all the mats and balls and set them up as your own personal playground, and he didn't get the dynamics of a group class. And he certainly didn't get the ideas of discipline and respect.

Joe and Jack came home one day after a particularly trying class, and my husband said, "I just can't watch him like that anymore." It was one of the few times I saw Joe emotionally distraught over Jack's limitations. We quit after two months.

Jack's not a big fan of organized athletics. Last fall we tried the adaptive soccer program (designed for kids with special needs), and although he possessed a modicum of skill, Jack hated it. Every weekend he began an anti-soccer campaign that started with offhand comments like "Soccer is bad for me" and "That field is bumpy." One of us always managed to coax him into the car, though on the drive there Jack gathered steam, bolstering his arguments by screeching, "It's too HOT out!" Eventually, whichever one of us was taking him on that particular day would trundle over to the field wearing a phony we-can-make-this-work-for-an-hour grin. It was painful. Sometimes Jack refused to play at all.

Midway through the season we sat him down and explained that he had to do *something*. Joe and I felt it was important to keep all of our kids active and especially wanted Jack to learn to regulate his body through some kind of organized movement. We gave him a choice: he could continue with soccer or we'd try karate again. He agreed to stick with soccer until the end of the season, but during the next game, in front of what seemed like every mother and father and uncle and teacher and grandparent in town, he sailed down the sideline kicking the ball and shouting, "I want to do KARATE INSTEAD!"

On that brilliantly sunny October afternoon it occurred to me: regardless of ability, concepts like competition and winning are nearly meaningless in Jack's mind. The idea of team dynamics, of passing a ball and scoring points is nearly foreign to a boy who, if left to his own devices, would choose to spend hours alone playing with a radio.

Still, our experience swimming at the Y had reinforced the value of Jack having a physical outlet, and we hadn't changed our minds about Jack participating in some kind of sport. At the end of the summer, as I started to organize our schedule of afterschool activities, we asked him again what he would like to choose that year.

"Karate."

Joe and I exchanged weary glances, anticipating long afternoons of cajoling him into his uniform and chasing him when we got there. Long afternoons of *put that ball back* and *sit with the others.*

"With all of us," he added. "With all of our kids."

Then it occurred to me: although Jack doesn't understand keeping score or competing for wins, he does understand family. He understands the idea of sticking together and playing fair. He understands that he feels good when his siblings are near him.

Joey and Charlie had been taking karate classes for over a year at the studio in town. When I approached the owner about the possibility of creating a "Cariello" class, with all five kids receiving instruction at once, he was thrilled with the idea. So were we.

When it came time for our first class, all five Cariello kids paraded in, clad in white, and within a few minutes they were imitating the kicks and punches and *ki-YA's* the instructor demonstrated for them. All five kids sat when they were told, stood when they needed to, and laughed out loud with each other. All five kids learned about discipline and respect.

What a difference three brothers and one sister make.

I was very moved by Jack's newfound love of martial arts and enjoyed watching our kids share an activity. It was good, clean fun all around.

But Joe couldn't leave well enough alone.

My husband suggested we take "Cariello Karate" to another level, a level where both he and I also participated, a level where he and I both donned gis, those outfits of crisp, white pants, elastic waistbands, and vest-y things that belt around the midsection. A level where he and I, along with our children, would also kick in the air and shout *ki-YA* at imaginary opponents.

I thought this was taking the whole love and loyalty and family thing just a smidge too far.

I resisted. I claimed fatigue. I brought up old cheerleading injuries (even though I'd never led a single cheer in my life). I told him it would diminish our parental authority to have our kids see us punching each other.

"Come on!" he wheedled. "Think how much fun it will be!"

Finally I broke down and admitted the real reason I couldn't do karate: the outfit. I would not be caught dead in that uniform. The billowy pants, the jacket that stops short of my wrists, the colorful belts—none of it worked for me. I am not a fashionista by any means, but I do understand what flatters a five-foot nine-inch, thirty-eight-year-old woman who has birthed more than forty pounds of people. And an entire outfit of monochrome cotton ain't it. Plus I do not wear white after Labor Day.

Joe had marshaled the kids in support of his mission. Now my entire family insisted that we all do this together, so I emailed the studio to ask if Joe and I might be included in the class. I was hoping they would say something about it being just for kids, about how parents were discouraged from getting involved. No such luck. Master Stewart wrote right back saying that "The family who practices together stays together," or some such nonsense.

And so, come two-thirty on a beautiful Friday afternoon, I climbed into my uniform and floated downstairs looking like a giant marshmallow. Jack took one glance at me and shouted, "You look WEIRD!" By the time we got to the studio the entire family was smirking in my direction, even three-year-old Henry.

I was the tiniest bit huffy about the whole thing, but being the good, generous sport that I am, I joined in and practiced with the kids.

During the middle of class, as I was watching Master Stewart demonstrate some punching move, I saw something colorful flash near the hem of his black uniform. I recognized it at once: the autism ribbon.

For the remainder of the session, as Rose punched and kicked and shouted *ki-YA* in my ear, I thought about what uniforms stand for. They stand for things like community and kinship. They stand for familiarity and unity. They say *I'm a part of this group* and *these people mean something to me* and *I believe in them.*

They stand for family.

With his carefully stitched ribbon positioned on the hem of his uniform, Master Stewart told me something significant. He told me *I may not understand the tantrums and the long wait to hear him speak and the fear that ran through your very soul like icy water down a smooth rock, but I will try.* He told me *Jack is welcome here* and *we accept him.* His ribbon said *you are not alone* and *now we are here together.*

I don't know what prompted Master Stewart to sew the symbol of autism on his own uniform—maybe he was touched by our family and others in the community like us. Perhaps someone in his own family was on the spectrum. Whatever the reason, his unspoken message was powerful and loud: we belong. Jack belongs. And for a family that has sometimes struggled to find a place in the community that speaks to each of us, where Jack's autism is understood and even valued, this means a great deal.

That's what a uniform can do, and now I am proud to wear one, too. Even after Labor Day.

A Letter to Rose ❧

Dear Rose,

Today you turned five, and it seems like the time has flown by so very fast. It feels like just yesterday when the nurse announced, "It's a girl!" and Daddy staggered in surprise. Just yesterday that I came home to paint a pale pink room with you by my side in the infant carrier. Just yesterday when our Rose started to bloom.

In the past five years you have blossomed into one of my most favorite people in the world. Your personality reminds me of the salted caramel candy we both love: for the most part sweet but with just enough sass to turn heads.

One Sunday evening Charlie was teasing you as we drove to Grandma and Grandpa's for dinner. You held up your fist menacingly and warned, "Charlie? When we get to Grandma's I'm going to hit you."

Sassy.

CARRIE CARIELLO

I overheard you playing with Jack a few weeks ago. As the both of you guided toy trains on a track, you remarked to him, "Know what, Jack? I love you. Just the way you are."

Sweet.

At the moment you love monkeys: monkey puzzles, monkey books, monkey clothes. You sleep underneath sheets patterned with monkeys wearing tiaras—a perfect combination.

Many people say your assertiveness comes from growing up with four boys, but I disagree. I've never known someone as sure of themselves, as self-possessed, as you. I'm certain you'd be the same true girl whether surrounded by a family of brothers or sisters. (Or monkeys.)

You are one part girly-girl and one part tough guy, all wrapped up in a delightfully rosy package. If given a choice, you'll pick trucks over dolls and plastic guns over princesses. But you want your trucks and guns pink. And you love getting your nails done, except you usually prefer them black or lime-green.

You like ketchup on everything.

You refuse to wear barrettes or headbands. Recently you were complaining about having your hair combed, and I suggested that maybe we shouldn't grow it long like Rapunzel after all, maybe we should trim it. "Yeah, sure," you said.

"Cut it all off. I don't care!"

You love to wrestle with the boys, and one night after dinner you challenged Grandpa to a boxing match. "Come on, Grandpa! Is that all you've got?"

The expression "Daddy's Girl" doesn't nearly do you justice. Every day, in your deep, raspy voice, you tell us that you want to marry Daddy, that you love him more than me. I

136

don't mind; I know it's your old need to forever see our family intact, to keep us all firmly rooted in your childhood.

People say you look like me, and sometimes I see my own mother resonating in your quick smile. But already your wispy blonde hair is thickening, darkening, changing. I suspect by the time you're a teenager you'll be more Cariello than Watterson.

Again, I don't mind. Because you may be your Daddy's girl, but you'll always be my daughter.

Happy birthday, my little flower.

Love,

Mom

Anxiety and Medication ❧

I NEVER THOUGHT I'D GET used to the fact that Jack is autistic.

I remember pushing a double stroller through our old neighborhood in Buffalo, and letting the word roll around in my mouth like the tiniest ball bearing: autism, autism, autism. My son has autism.

But before long the word and the diagnosis both became ordinary parts of who he was. I got used to it, the same way I got used to the fierce public tantrums and the way he needed to watch particular *Baby Einstein* movies to soothe his distress. And the more I got used to Jack and his autism, the more I came to love them both.

Over the years Jack has struggled with a variety of behaviors that Joe and I worked him through. Ranging from dangerous (getting up early and turning on the coffee machine) to merely annoying (clicking the doors open and shut throughout the house), each phase seemed to end almost the very second we couldn't take it anymore. For two months straight he wiped soap all over the walls. For a while he was fixated on flushing the toilet over and over, and then he wanted to listen to a certain song all day long. We were always able to work him through whatever it was. Or else we just hid the soap.

In January 2011, Jack's behavior started to change more dramatically. He was afraid of ordinary things like going to the grocery store or using the bathroom. Sometimes when we were in the car he would scream and bang his head if I had to make a right turn. His sleep was often interrupted, and we heard him tossing and rocking all night long.

He started having imaginary conversations with himself, gesturing wildly and pointing his finger. One night I was sitting with him as he launched into one of these exchanges, and I couldn't help but think to myself that he looked crazy. I begged him to tell me who he was talking to and what he was saying, but he never responded, never broke out of his internal dialogue. It was as though he never even heard me.

At school they were as mystified as we were. One day Jack told his teacher, "The baby will paint me blue. I am afraid." Or he would launch into a tirade and scream, "I hate them all! I hate my friends!" and beg to go home. After his outburst we had an emergency meeting with his team and his teacher to talk about what could be triggering him, if perhaps anything in the classroom or at home had changed and somehow set him off. But none of us could trace his behavior to a particular event or instance; we were all at a loss.

And then, like sunshine appearing in the middle of a storm, he'd have a few good days, and we'd relax. It's just a phase like always, we told ourselves. He'll get through it.

In the midst of these symptoms I was training to run a half-marathon with a group of friends. The race was scheduled for the middle of February in Orlando, and I was worried about leaving Jack because he seemed so emotionally fragile. Several times I changed my flight times to shorten the trip and minimize how long I'd be away. Joe continually assured me that he would be fine handling things.

"You need the break," he told me.

While I was away in sunny Florida, Joe cared for all the kids back in snowy New Hampshire. I returned to find Joe stricken, deeply concerned after three straight days with Jack. Joe told me it was time we did something about his worsening issues. He wondered how we let things go for so long, and I remember him saying, "It's like we're losing him all over again."

I guess I just got used to it.

Joe's despair propelled us into action. I realized this wasn't one of Jack's many phases, a set of new issues he would outgrow just before we couldn't take it any longer. This was more.

I made a list of all the changes we'd noticed for the past month. Here is an excerpt from my handwritten notes:

He's not sleeping. He falls asleep okay but wakes in the night and again around four, then rocks in bed.

He talks to himself constantly. Seems to be carrying on a conversation with someone in his head. Looks angry, with his face often contorting into pained expressions. He's starting to do this daily.

Terrified of going to the bathroom alone, he's having several accidents a week; especially has trouble with bowel movements. Shrieks and rocks when he has to go.

Rarely engages with the family. He hangs on the periphery, often circling the room or standing in the doorway watching all of us. This is driving Joe crazy.

He whines constantly, is always in distress. Doesn't like taking right turns in the car and is afraid of the wind-chill factor and the blue water in the toilet bowl. He talks a lot about babies. He asks about the temperature outside at least three dozen times a day. Has no joy in any activities he used to enjoy, things like coloring, Wii, music, baking with me.

He rarely smiles or laughs out loud.

Looking over my notes a few days after I'd written them, I started to put the pieces in place and finally saw what Jack had been struggling with for over a month: anxiety. Never having experienced acute anxiety myself, it took this list for me to fully comprehend his month-long change in behavior and temperament. Though we didn't know why—and perhaps never would—Jack was suddenly anxious about nearly everything.

We scrambled to make appointments with a variety of specialists: our developmental pediatrician, a behavioralist, and a pediatric psychiatrist. Unfortunately, all of them were booked months in advance and couldn't see us right away, so (not wanting to wait) we made an appointment with our regular pediatrician. Joe took the morning off from work so we could both bring Jack.

Rattled with fear and anxiety on the drive to the office, Jack noticeably relaxed the second we sat down in the exam room to wait for the doctor. He stopped begging to check the temperature on Joe's phone, and he spoke in normal tones about school and lunch. He smiled when Joe threatened to tickle him. Joe and I locked eyes, astonished at the sudden change but excited to see that our little boy was still there underneath all the anguish.

The doctor came in, and we reviewed Jack's symptoms while our son quietly traced his finger along the outlines of a large wall mural. The doctor—who's known Jack since he was three—nodded knowingly and confirmed that, yes, we were dealing with anxiety. At one point I motioned to Jack and commented on his calmness, how different he seemed at the moment. "Does he seem anxious to you?" I asked. "Absolutely," he answered. "You can tell just by looking at him."

Wow, I thought. Imagine if he'd seen him an hour ago

when we were trying to get him in the car. Even in a calmer state Jack was still acting nervous, distraught, worried.

The doctor went on to explain how anxiety and autism typically go hand-in-hand and recommended that we consider medication. Both Joe and I flinched. We know there is no real "test" for evaluating anxiety, that medical practitioners typically assess the presenting symptoms and then diagnose this tricky disorder, but this felt too fast. Although not holistic by any means, we weren't prepared to put Jack on daily medication if we could find something else to alleviate his symptoms. Emotionally, turning to medication so quickly felt like a failure, as though we hadn't solved the problem but would only be masking the symptoms. And we couldn't imagine having him taking anti-anxiety medicine every single day, potentially for the rest of his life.

Nodding his head along as we argued our case, the doctor suggested that we take the prescription with us anyway, and use it if we changed our minds.

Medication seemed like a last resort to us, and Joe and I resolved to explore alternate methods to help Jack cope. For the next few weeks we focused all of our energy on reducing our son's anxiety and helping him move past the debilitating fear that now controlled his life.

Joe's sister, Elaine, is a professional in special education and suggested a brushing technique called the Wilbarger Protocol to help lessen Jack's anxiety. Created by Patricia Wilbarger in 1991, the regimen is designed to reduce sensory defensiveness by using a small white brush with flexible bristles to apply pressure on the limbs and back periodically throughout the day. I approached Jack's team at school with the idea, and our occupational therapist spent a morning training me on how to stroke Jack's body with long, firm movements. We created a schedule where we "brushed" him hourly. For a month, the occupational therapist brushed him at school, and Joe and I took turns doing it at home. However, even though Jack enjoyed the feeling, it never really seemed to alleviate his symptoms.

We also created (or re-created) social stories for nearly every activity in Jack's life: boarding the bus, sitting for lunch, having a bowel movement. Still he held the school bus up every morning by refusing to step on, could barely sit long enough to eat a sandwich, and had accidents in his pants. Still he whined and fussed both day and night. Still he talked to himself.

Still he was anxious.

At this point it was March, and these long three months took a toll on our family. Joey and Charlie share a room with Jack, and his restlessness was affecting their sleep. Charlie, especially, seemed troubled by the change in his older brother—he would try to encourage Jack to come and sit at the table or play with him more often than usual. We all became worried, watchful.

As a mother I'd never felt more fragile. After the half-marathon in Orlando I'd switched over to Bikram Yoga, and each morning I wept as I drove downtown to class, thinking about how scared I was that Jack would never get better, that

I would never again see the happy little boy who had disappeared underneath these layers of distress.

We hit rock bottom one chilly night at the end of March. Not having planned dinner, we decided to take the kids out to eat at a casual restaurant in town. They were excited for this mid-week treat and chatted animatedly on the drive there—except for Jack, who withdrew and dozed a bit in the warm car. As soon as we pulled in he announced he could not get out. While Joe walked the other four in and got them seated, I all but dragged Jack through the cold parking lot and into the lobby of the restaurant. He started to scream and bang his head with his fists, insisting he could not stay, he had to leave. While other guests and employees looked on, I desperately tried to convince him that he could do this, that everyone was hungry and we needed to sit down. After ten minutes I gave up, signaling to Joe that I couldn't budge him.

Joe switched places with me, and as I sat with the other kids I could see him slowly working Jack around the lobby, showing him pictures on the wall and helping him look through the menu. Little by little I watched as Jack's body relaxed and he let Joe put his arm around his shoulders. At long last they approached the table, and Jack slumped in the seat next to me.

"I'll have soup," he said.

And although this anecdote could be considered a success story—we got him to sit with us and eat, after all—we were continually feeling drained by the sheer effort it took to get Jack through each day. From peeing in the morning to showering at night, every move had become a slow, tortuous crawl through the muddy waters of his anxiety.

On the car ride home from the restaurant, we decided to fill the prescription.

The doctor had counseled us that if the medicine was going to work, it would work right away, and if it didn't, we could stop anytime. The very next night we doled out half of a tiny white pill, and we held our breath. It took just a few days to build up in his system, and by the end of the week Jack began the ascent out of his pit of despair. He returned to us.

About a year after our experience with Jack's anxiety, Joe went through a very rough period of his own. He'd just purchased his second dental practice, and things hadn't gone as smoothly as they had for him the first time. As with Jack's anxiety, Joe couldn't sleep, his mind working constantly. He dropped about thirty pounds over the course of only six weeks, and for the second time I watched, powerless, as someone I loved circled the deep, dark hole of anxiety.

Luckily, Joe could identify his feelings and communicate his needs. He could take steps to help himself. But it was eye-opening for both of us to see first-hand just what Jack must have felt like during those long months. We regretted holding out on medication for as long as we did.

And now? Well, it really is amazing what you can get used to. Once opposed to daily medication, now every night before bed we holler out, "Jack! You need your PILL!"

But Jack smiles every day now. And that is something I will never get too used to.

Cariello Cruise ✌

LAST SPRING JOE AND I DECIDED it was finally time to take a family vacation. For the past nine years we'd been either pregnant or caring for an infant (often both), and except for the annual family reunion in New Jersey, we'd never traveled with all five kids.

After some research we chose to go on a Disney Cruise, mostly because of the youth clubs they offered, where you can drop your kids off and actually enjoy some time alone. When I called to book the trip, the Disney agent said to me in a Paula Deen-like southern accent, "There's just one thing, ho-ney. You ain't goin' to see your kids at *awl*." I couldn't get my credit card out fast enough.

The cruise promised to be a dream vacation aboard a ship coincidentally named the *Disney Dream*. It promised the perfect combination of sun-filled days with the kids and candle-lit nights as a couple. We would be charmed by

Mickey and awed by the service, and by the last day Cruella De Vil herself would have to drag us off that giant vessel kicking and screaming.

Now, I know what you're thinking. "Don't you have a son with autism?" you're asking. "And isn't he a tad bit inflexible?"

Yes, we do. But fortunately, Jack is the sort of kid who likes adventure and he's relatively unruffled even if we change things up or switch our routine around, especially if we tell him about it first and include things like social stories so he knows what to expect. He loves staying in hotels and eating in restaurants, and every year he begs us to fly somewhere. He loves water slides and swimming.

What he hates are mascots. People in costume. Characters with big wobbly heads and oversized feet.

Knowing this, Joe and I strategized about how to prepare him for the cruise and all of the Disney characters on the ship. We decided to emphasize the parts of the cruise that Jack would enjoy most—like the pools and the endless ice cream—and use social stories to help him manage his fears, like the giant mouse and the giant duck.

I recently read over my daily journal from around that time; here's what I found:

Wednesday, February 15, 2012
We booked the Disney cruise today. When I announced the total cost Joe collapsed face down on the couch. And I hadn't even factored in the airfare yet. We set sail at the end of June—best to wait a little longer to tell the kids.

Thursday, May 3rd

Mickey Mouse called the house to announce the cruise to the kids. They went nuts. Henry started running in circles around the kitchen, arms raised and fists pumping, shouting, "We're going to Disney! We're going to Disney! I have to poop! I have to POOP NOW!"

Right away Jack started asking about the Disney characters. How big are they? Do they talk? We reassured him that the characters are really just people in costume, nothing more. He asked if they lived on other planets, too.

Wednesday, June 20th

Packing begins. I've run all over town, determined to find five matching red suitcases, five matching neon yellow t-shirts, and five matching fluorescent bathing suits. We will be hard to miss.

Saturday, June 23rd

Jack is nervous. He's very excited about the trip, but today he started exhibiting his classic signs of anxiety: nervous pacing, wild gesturing, and overall restlessness. I came into the kitchen in time to see him animatedly jabbing his finger in the air while muttering. I asked him who he was talking to, and he said, "Nikki." I thought maybe he meant "Mickey," as in mouse, but when I pressed him further he repeated, "Nikki." We don't know a Nikki, so I asked him who she was. "I can't tell you. No one. Don't ask," he said.

Now I'm nervous.

Sunday, June 24th

Long day of travel. We left the house at six-fifteen in the morning to head to the airport and arrived in Orlando about twelve-thirty. Stood for a long time at the baggage carousel trying to identify our red suitcases amongst all the other red suitcases. Turns out red is a popular color for luggage. Joe couldn't stop smirking.

Took a car service to the port where the Disney Dream was docked. Jack kept asking our driver, Leo, if he had a driver's license. "Do you even know how to drive, Leo?" he demanded, agitated by this last leg of the trip.

At last, amid much fanfare and music, we boarded the cruise ship. The kids are thrilled, even Jack. He is, however, keeping a watchful eye for wandering characters, and we heard him chanting, "Just humans in costume, just humans in costume," under his breath.

Monday, June 25th

This morning before breakfast I brought Rose downstairs to the Grand Lobby for the scheduled appearance of the Disney princesses. Eyes shining, she took in the scene of glittery dresses and sparkling tiaras. When I suggested we hop in line to get her picture taken, Rose turned to me and in her husky voice said, "Nah. Let's go eat breakfast with the boys instead." I agreed with my delightful girl; I'll take syrupy pancakes over syrupy princesses any day.

Today we took an excursion off the ship to the Disney-owned island, Castaway Cay. All five kids were excited to swim in the Caribbean and catch hermit crabs. They had lunch with the youth club on the island while Joe and I took a long walk to the adults-only beach. (I think Joe thought "adults-only" meant topless; he seemed disappointed at the usual variety of multicolored tankinis.) I read and took a long nap. Love vacation!

Tuesday, June 26th
This morning we docked at Paradise Island in the Bahamas and left the ship to tour the Atlantis resort, an enormous place with hotels, coves, and beaches. The main attraction for the Cariello clan was the 150-acre water park, complete with a slide that ran right through a giant shark tank. However, as we rode the rickety Bahamian shuttle over the bridge toward the resort, the overcast day turned ominously dark. Keeping one eye on the sky, we followed our tour guide through the gardens and fish ponds of the estate-like property. Before we were through the tour, the skies suddenly opened up, releasing sheets of rain.

And then, as quickly as it had begun, the downpour ceased. We Cariellos were shaken. And wet. But we jollied along and headed to the water park where we changed into our bathing suits. After all, we told the kids, we were wet already! (And we'd paid already!)

The water park was massive, with a wave pool, several enormous slides, a lazy river, and an area created to look like an abandoned ship where kids could play. That's where I set up shop with the younger kids while Joe took the older boys around to the larger attractions.

During the afternoon I lost Jack. He was there one minute and gone the next, just like they tell you. I felt physically sick as I circled the wading pool, searching, searching, searching for him. My heart was pounding. How would we ever find him? He could be anywhere in this massive resort.

My eyes darted back and forth as I balanced myself between a mother's concern and full-blown panic. At last I glimpsed his bright yellow bathing suit weaving in and out of the crowd. I charged up to him, scolding and hugging and asking where he'd been, where he'd gone.

He answered nonchalantly, "I wanted to see things. I'm a big boy now." Turns out he'd gone on a water slide. Alone. (Well, I'm assuming Nikki went too, but still. She's not shaping up to be much of a chaperone.) I started to cry.

Shortly before lunchtime, Joe took Joey and Jack over to the lazy river while I stayed with the younger kids near the play area. Once again thick clouds rolled in, this time accompanied by loud cracks of thunder. Lifeguards cleared the pool area and parents quickly gathered up their children. My kids were frantic, especially Charlie, but I decided the best thing was to stay put so Joe would know where to find us. We huddled under an umbrella while rain streamed down around us and lightening lit up the sky.

This is a vacation? I thought to myself. *Thousands of*

dollars to crouch under an umbrella and sing "You are my Sunshine" over and over so my kids don't freak out in the middle of a torrential downpour? They never mentioned this in the brochure.

Finally Joe returned, the two older boys in tow. I could barely hear him over the rain, but he motioned for us to follow him. Jack and Joey were both wide-eyed, and Jack had his hands clapped over his ears to block out the cracks of thunder. Holding Henry in one arm and Rose in the other, Joe raced through the sidewalks in search of cover while the rest of us ran after him. As I ran, my street clothes fell out of the beach bag and were instantly soaked. I bundled them quickly back into the bag and raced after my family.

Then, in a single instant, the world around us turned blindingly white. In that same instant I was certain I had been struck by lightning. In the booming aftermath of the thunder that followed, my ears and throat burned. I couldn't stop shaking. The little kids were screaming, and Charlie was pale. For a brief moment, it was as if the world was on fire.

When the rain let up we regrouped for the second time in three hours. At this point everyone was hungry and distraught, so we decided to change back into dry clothes and try to calm the kids down over lunch. (I stayed in my suit since my regular clothes were now drenched. Sigh.)

Finally calm and now munching on burgers and fries (thankfully indoors), we could see one of Atlantis' main attractions, that giant shark tank with the clear water slide running through it. Before the long, hellish morning of tropical downpours and lighting strikes, Joe and I had discussed bringing Joey and maybe Charlie down that slide. Given that Jack generally avoids animals of any kind, we figured he wouldn't be interested.

When we were done eating we all walked over to admire the sharks and to watch people ride inner tubes down the tank's slide. Weary, still a bit damp, and suspicious of even more dark clouds on the horizon, Joe and I quietly agreed to just head back to the ship. As we turned around and started to usher the kids back outside, we heard a determined voice in a familiar tone.

"I will go on that slide."

Jack. Standing with his hands splayed on the glass and his eyes fixed on the sharks circling the glass tube, he looked back at us and repeated, "I will go. On that slide."

Enough said. If my autistic son—who once threw up when he glimpsed a Chihuahua sitting in the front seat of a car—wants to glide on an inner tube through a tank full of sharks, I'm not going to stand in his way. I took Jack and Joey to the restroom where they quickly changed back into their suits, then we grabbed three tubes and I took my two oldest boys to the ride.

I hate water slides. I hate the twists and the turns and the cold rush of water on my face. And I hate them even more when they're dark and enclosed. I especially hate them when sharks are involved. But I felt like I should be a big girl for my big boy.

The line was shorter than I expected, so I didn't have much time to prepare myself before we found ourselves at the front. I took a few deep breaths and then slid down right after Jack into the twisty, turning, wet, shark-y tunnel. I could hear my boys whooping the whole way down.

It was the sound of vacation.

Tuesday Night (still June 26th)

After such a trying day, we sent the kids to the Disney club for the evening. Over a quiet dinner and a much-needed cocktail, Joe and I talked about the events at Atlantis. I still felt very distraught about nearly losing Jack, and I knew the memory would revisit me tonight when I tried to sleep. Joe reassured me that in Jack's mind he wasn't lost—he knew right where he was the whole time. This led to a conversation about Jack's theory of mind, and how wandering off to a water slide is an example of his inflexible thinking. Because he knew where he was, he assumed we knew where he was, too.

It's clear that as Jack grows, he's beginning to crave independence. At home I've noticed he wants to do things like cut his own piece of cake or serve himself at the table. "I can do it! I'm good at it!" His autism will continue to provide challenges as he matures, and the combination of inflexible thinking and his emerging desire for independence will require us to be even more watchful than before.

Wednesday, June 27th

Day at sea. We spent a lot of time on the top deck enjoying the pools and the large "Aqua Duck" water slide, a huge tube that circles the top deck of the ship. The kids love it, and Jack in particular can't get enough of it. Only problem is that every time chubby Henry—even plumper now from mornings of Mickey-shaped waffles and afternoons of Mickey-shaped ice cream bars—sees a cloud, he shrieks and runs for his Crocs. "I need my cwocs! Give me my cwocs and take me inside! Thunder! *Wightening!*"

I'm not sure which makes me feel worse; his new thunderstorms phobia or the fact that the Crocs make his kankles look even bigger and more kankly.

Shrieking aside, a fun and relaxing day.

Just before dinner we posed with two characters from *The Incredibles*, both decked out in identical superhero costumes. At the last second Jack agreed to stand with our family for the picture.

Pretty incredible.

Thursday, June 28th

Back to Castaway Cay for time on the beach. The kids had a ball with still more swimming and hermit crabs. We all enjoyed a barbecue lunch together and then returned to the ship late in the afternoon. Once we were back on board, Joey begged to go to the kids' club for the evening. We were suspicious of his enthusiasm; turned out he had met a girl there.

Our spirits were buoyed. Maybe we'll marry one of these kids off yet—they're never too young to start thinking about it. We sent them all to the club for the night in the hopes they'd each meet a future spouse.

Joe and I ate in the adult dining room and had the best chocolate soufflé ever.

New to the cruise scene, Joe and I didn't realize until the last minute that we were expected to disembark by seven-thirty the following morning. Our Jamaican server's hearty "See you breakfast at six forty-five!" tipped us off that something was amiss. We scrambled through our documents and discovered, in teeny-tiny print, that Disney wanted us off the boat early so they could load up the next group. Not a big deal, except that our plane wasn't scheduled to leave until two-thirty in the afternoon. That meant more airport hours than we'd planned on, and an airport is not the ideal place to keep five kids entertained.

Friday, June 29th

On the way to the airport, Joe decided to call Jet Blue to check if we could get on an earlier flight. Miracle of miracles, they had seven seats available on the nine-twenty, meaning that we would be saved from having to keep five small people amused in an airport for six hours—but only if we could manage to get those same small people (one of whom had just decided that "I a puppy now! I only crawl on the floor!") through check-in and airport security in just half an hour.

Seven pairs of shoes off at security, five red suitcases to be checked, four kids, and a "puppy" to keep focused and moving. Joe and I were both sweating.

We made it.

Given our last-minute flight change, it was no surprise that our seats were not all together. The three older boys ended up sitting separately in the middle seats of different rows, each child flanked by two strangers. We had three adjacent seats near the back of the plane where Joe could sit with Rose and Henry. In the chaos and shuffle, I managed to score a seat alone two rows behind him.

As we headed down the runway I worried about the boys flying by themselves, halfway up the aisle from us. When the seatbelt light went off I rushed to check on them. They were fine. Each sported a pair of silver wings on their shirts, courtesy of the flight attendant, and they were enjoying large sodas and cookies.

Jack introduced me to his seatmate. "This is Hannah. She has a Diet Coke and a cup with three ice cubes in it." I glanced over at Hannah—who refused to meet my eye—and suggested to Jack that maybe he'd like to switch seats with the person next to me, who had graciously offered to move for us. Then we could sit together.

"No. I'm a big boy now."

I scurried back down the aisle to my own seat, where I settled back in with my own Diet Coke and finished my book. In between chapters I asked the flight attendant if she could tell the dark-haired man two rows ahead of me to please keep his children quiet as they were being very disruptive.

Friday Afternoon (still June 29th)
Home at last. Joe collapsed face down on the couch again while five yellow-clad children dragged in one red suitcase apiece.

All in all, a successful trip. One giant leap for our family, a few small steps for a big boy with autism. And a free vacation for Nikki.

A Letter to Charlie ❧

Dear Charlie,

Today you turned six, and over the course of one year you've lost the roundness of a five-year-old and become all knees and elbows.

Out of all of the kids, you resemble Daddy the most. You're both slow to anger and quick to laugh, and both of you have deep brown eyes that flash alike in joy and in temper. You have his dark hair.

The special gift you bring to our family is your ability to teach, to show, to explain. One day I asked you to unbuckle Henry from his car seat for me, and you answered, "Mom, I'll show him how to do it so he can try it next time." Patiently you stood by him while the rest of us filed into the house, guiding his chubby fingers over the buckles until at last he released the button. Both of you shouted for joy.

This past year you went through a time where you were plagued by nightmares, night after night crawling into our bed for comfort. Night after night we walked you back to your room and tucked you snugly under your covers with the promise that you were safe, that there were no monsters. Eventually you outgrew this phase, but a small part of me misses your nocturnal visits, those wide brown eyes shining in the dark.

Your nickname is "Charlie-Bear" or "Brown Bear," because you are warm and soft and dark, exactly like a little baby bear cub.

In the fall you started kindergarten at the same school Joey and Jack go to. After a few weeks you noticed Jack had an aide or, in your words, "a girl who walks around with him and makes sure he doesn't get lost." You seemed to accept this as ordinary. Although Jack's diagnosis remains unnamed for you at this point, I know you sense he's different, unusual. I can see it in the way you anticipate his needs and take special care in communicating with him. "Jack. Dog. On a leash. You're safe." It won't be long before you unlock the mystery and realize Jack has autism.

You are exceptionally attached to Joey; your relationship is unlike anything I've ever seen. You play together, sleep together, breathe together. Nothing seems real for either of you until you've shared it, and the sound of your voices shouting and giggling echoes through the house all day. You love a good joke, and you have an infectious laugh that comes from deep within.

You are athletic and naturally inclined to sports. Nothing makes you happier than a game of catch in the yard or a family bike ride after dinner. This year you played baseball and surprised the coach with your hitting ability.

As the middle child, you're able to play with any one of the kids at any given time: Legos with Joey, scooters with Jack, monkey puzzles with Rose, blocks with Henry. You were born to be in a big family; you thrive in the chaos and commotion, and appear lonesome whenever you're on your own.

Some days you remind me of an old man trapped in a little boy's body; you tend to be anxious, worrisome. Dark clouds on the horizon make you panic, loud noises send you running, and you fear the sight of blood. But as soon as Joey tells a joke to make you laugh, the storm clouds lift from your eyes, and I get an affirming glimpse of my joyful, spirited little boy, my Charlie-bear.

Happy Birthday.

Love,

Mom

Believe and Breathe ❧

I WAS BAKING COOKIES with the kids on a snowy December afternoon in 2009 when my friend Pam called and asked me to join a charity team that was running the Boston Marathon for the Doug Flutie Jr. Foundation for Autism. I agreed, mostly because I wanted to get back to eating my macaroons without interruption, but also because it seemed boorish to turn the offer down when my own child was on the spectrum.

Before I could say "biscotti," Pam had dropped off a crazy-looking training schedule, and I was off and running. Literally.

My journey to the Boston Marathon actually started long before Pam's call. It began on a particularly low Saturday back in November 2007, when Jack was just three. After relocating to New Hampshire less than a year earlier, life with him remained uncertain and tumultuous. We were still learning to accept the daily challenges of life with a child on the spectrum—alarms on the doors in case he escaped, a lock on the refrigerator to keep him from experimenting with eggs, for example—and we regularly tried new tactics to diffuse the outbursts that often put our household in a tailspin.

On this chilly gray afternoon I was paying for a haircut when I noticed a display of inexpensive necklaces at the front desk of the salon. They had little words like "Dream" or "Peace" inscribed around the edge of a small silver circlet, and a thin chain running through it so it would hang easily around your neck. I saw one engraved with "Believe" and thought, why not? I could use a tangible reminder of my commitment to soldiering on and believing.

The next day something thrilling happened with this inexpensive piece of silver. We were at a birthday party for a friend of Jack's, and he was in the throes of one of his legendary tantrums. Out of desperation I held the small circle up and asked him, "What does Mommy's necklace say?" He focused on it just long enough for me to say, "Believe. It says believe, Jack, because I believe in you." He turned his blue eyes up to meet mine and mouthed "Believe" and the tantrum was over.

Over the course of the next year he and I both turned to that exchange to calm ourselves if he started to spin out of control. Repeated more than a hundred times by now, our dialogue is unchanged.

"What does Mommy's necklace say?"

Unfailingly he answers, "Believe, because I believe in you."

Quite a while has passed since I bought that necklace, and during this time Jack has developed into a different boy entirely. He can hold a conversation, share a joke, and ask appropriate questions. Still I wear the necklace faithfully. I wear it if I know we'll be in a situation that's challenging for Jack and I'll need some strength to get us both through.

My training for the marathon was everything you would expect, given that I was trying to get a body that's birthed five children to run 26.2 miles without collapsing or failing in some embarrassing way (think "runner's trots"). It was exhilarating and frustrating, challenging and rewarding. That spring much of my life revolved around a training schedule that toggled between short and long runs. It felt like I had committed to a running program created by Kenyans, for Kenyans. There were days I wanted to cry. Cry when my children asked why I was even doing this race when there wasn't a chance I would win it. Cry when the thermometer hung below freezing on a day scheduled for a long run. And cry, cry, cry as I watched my spiteful scale jump up a pound or two after spending a week putting more miles on my body than on my car. (Kenyans apparently don't carbo-load with Oreos.)

Before I knew it, race day was upon me. I thought I was ready, felt prepared to go the distance. I'd kept to the training schedule religiously and sailed through a twenty-mile race back in March. Completing the marathon should be no problem at all.

I was wrong.

Although I did everything I could to prepare for that day, the race course owned me from the very first mile. I was unused to the bobbing and weaving one had to do to get through the crowds of runners, while at the same time trying to find my own rhythm. Plus, the ice cream sundae I'd foolishly enjoyed the night before kept my stomach on high alert.

I hit the first wall at mile seven when my right hip announced its annoyance. I hit another at mile fifteen when my left hip got jealous and started making noise, too. But I really, really hit the big wall at mile twenty-two when I heard bystanders shouting out that there were only four miles to go. Only four miles? It sounded like I still had to run to the Statue of Liberty and back.

But just then something special happened. A spectator—someone I didn't even know—stepped in front of me, looked directly into my eyes, and said, "I believe in you."

This moment was a profound turning point at the end of a long journey. With just those four words—the same four words I use with my autistic son—this unknown man was telling me everything I needed to hear.

There are no accidents. It's no accident that I have a son named Jack who will forever interpret the world differently than most. It was no accident that I reached for a necklace that would reaffirm my faith in myself as a mother of a child with autism. And it was no accident that a stranger in a crowd of strangers spoke his mantra to me at a pivotal time in a hard-run race.

I've always believed in Jack. Now I believe in myself, too.

I continued running for about another year. I did a few half-marathons and was working on improving my speed, but then my body started talking back to me. A trip to the doctor confirmed what most people already know: too much running is terrible for your body. The perpetual pounding combined with the constant pressure on your joints can really wreak havoc over time, and apparently people who have birthed over forty pounds of children pay a special price. My pelvis was considered "unstable" by medical experts, and I was advised to significantly cut back on my mileage.

Although I'd only been running seriously for about two years, I'd already developed a not-so-healthy addiction commonly seen in running circles, this constant quest for the "runner's high." I needed to run every day, and anything less than five miles barely seemed worth getting out of bed for. I'd run through shin splints, nausea, and plain old fatigue. I'd run on Christmas Eve, New Year's Day, and Easter. It was a great way for me to clear my head and, frankly, to be alone for a bit.

But alas, I needed to find something else. Since I didn't relish the idea of undergoing a pelvic transplant, I decided it was time to hang up the sneakers and pursue a different form of exercise. (Hey, I wasn't giving up that hour of "me time!" I'm not crazy!) I'd heard about a new kind of yoga, called

Bikram, that was becoming quite popular, and I decided to give it a try, hoping to stretch out my tired body with this new form of exercise.

For those of you unfamiliar with the Bikram practice, it's a series of twenty-six postures and two breathing exercises that are performed in a hot room over ninety minutes. The practice was first designed by Chodbury Bikram, an Indian man in his sixties who struggled with an injury from weight lifting and so decided to develop a yoga practice to better connect his mind and body. The poses and the dialogue are exactly the same for each and every class around the world.

Like most Bikram beginners, I was a little hung up on the heat. Bikram is practiced in a humid room set at 105 degrees. I can barely take a hot summer day in New Hampshire without complaining, never mind sweating it out for ninety straight minutes in a moist, overheated room while balancing on one leg and worrying what everyone else is thinking about me. But the local Bikram websites all boasted a host of benefits, many of them related to flexibility and stretching, so I figured I'd give it a try.

I knew I was in trouble when the teacher checked me into the class and, upon realizing it was my first time, counseled me to "just breathe and stay in the room." *What? You're telling me it's going to be so hot that simply* breathing *is considered successful?*

That first class was crazy hot. As in you-must-be-a-crazy-person-to-be-here hot. But I stayed in the room. And breathed. In fact, I managed slightly more than that, stumbling my way through the seemingly foreign postures while sweat streamed down my face and my full-length yoga pants glued themselves to my sticky legs.

The next day I returned to that same hot, humid room for another class, and then again the following day. By the end of the first week I was hooked. I started to crave the daily sweat session and felt antsy if more than a day went by without visiting the studio.

It's difficult to describe to a newcomer how relaxing and exhilarating the walk back to your car can be after ninety minutes in a Bikram session. How you stand a little taller and your step is a little lighter. How the fact that lice are spreading through your son's third-grade classroom isn't quite so stressful anymore. More than once I've spent the fifteen-minute drive to the studio seething about an argument I've had with Joe or a fight with one of the kids over a last-minute homework assignment that didn't quite get finished, all while gripping the steering wheel and plotting my escape. (In most cases I've even worked out the custody arrangements: all five kids would live with Joe full-time in some teensy apartment he found on Craig's list, while I remained in our newly reno-vated house and took the kids every other weekend for fun outings like to the movies or the water park. The minute Joe picked them back up on Sunday night, I would clean the house and then kick back in peaceful solitude.)

After an hour and a half in the hot room, though, I always emerged with the knots slowly untangling in my mind.

Bikram yoga focuses as much on healing and

strengthening the mind as it does on the body. Yogis are encouraged to exercise stillness as they move in and out of the postures and to keep their minds free of thoughts unrelated to the work at hand. Bikram teaches mindfulness: a state of active, open attention to the present.

Not so easy for a wound-up chatterbox like myself.

No matter how hard I work to clear the clutter of grocery lists, deadlines, and breakfast negotiations from my mind, I struggle during every class to achieve that sense of stillness. I'd much rather watch what everyone else is doing, to maybe ask where they buy those hip yoga clothes. (I still don't know, but apparently it's not Walmart where mine come from.) And then there's that incessant internal dialogue I always seem to have: *can it get any hotter in here when will she put the fan on why did I wear these shorts I'm hungry that man in front of me sure is sweating why is she picking at that scab boy I'm really hot I hate these shorts.*

After nearly two years of practicing, I continue to have a hard time freeing myself from the mental binds of daily life and giving myself over to yoga's sacred movements. Despite my herculean efforts, remaining mindful for each and every yoga class is close to impossible. But every now and again I experience an advanced state of quiet, of mindfulness. I think of this state as one of reflection. For me, reflection is where I can transcend both the heat and noise in my head to consider important aspects of my life, mind, and body.

During a particularly warm class last fall I was happily nestled in one of those too rare reflective states of mind.

The teacher's voice was calm and soothing, and my body was moving easily from posture to posture. As I listened to the instructions I had a fascinating thought: yoga has a lot in common with autism. I began to notice strong parallels between my practice and my life with Jack.

During my first Bikram class I felt as though I'd alighted in a foreign land, a land where the natives are dressed in brightly patterned Lycra shorts and the leaders interspersed Sanskrit phrases between commands to touch our foreheads to the floor. I've known how to place my feet on the pavement and run since I was a small girl, but the movement and dialogue of yoga were entirely unfamiliar. I didn't have the right clothes, I couldn't understand the language, and my body felt too large and clunky for the graceful poses. The room smelled funny. I was overwhelmed, and my first response was to bolt from the studio without a backwards glance.

That first class gave me a valuable glimpse into what Jack faces everyday as he navigates through our world, a world with rules and regulations blurred by autism. I imagine that in his world the commands are as confusing to him as the instructions for Awkward Pose first were to me. (And really, that posture is confusing. And awkward.) It reminded me to consider our world from *his* vantage point.

I can leave uncomfortable places like the yoga studio at any time, but Jack can never leave our world or his autism behind. He likely always feels like a stranger in a confusing place.

One of the instructors at my studio often reminds us to find our *drishti*, or "focused gaze," during class, a technique used to develop concentration. And although *drishti* varies from posture to posture, students are often encouraged to make eye contact with themselves in the room's front mirror. This is not easy; for whatever reason, I find it much easier to evaluate my thighs than to make eye contact with myself, and I feel very uncomfortable meeting my own gaze for longer than a few seconds. I'm even more uncomfortable having someone repeatedly encouraging me to "Make eye contact."

The phrase, of course, is not new to me. Ever since Jack was a year old we've been urging (and sometimes commanding) him to make eye contact with us, often upwards of a dozen times in a single morning. In her book *Thinking in Pictures*, autistic author Temple Grandin explains that people on the spectrum avoid eye contact because they're disturbed by the movements of other people's eyes. After trying to meet my own eyes in the mirror during a Bikram yoga session, I can relate.

Another aspect of yoga I struggle with is *anticipating*, the bad habit I have of moving faster than the teacher's instruction and beginning a pose earlier than the rest of class. Because every Bikram session is exactly the same, with the same postures and timing, this is a very easy thing to do if I'm not mindful of waiting. Many times I've been gently reminded to stop anticipating, to instead move through the sequence with the rest of the class.

My instinct to anticipate in class mimics the same anticipation I have for Jack's future. Ever since he was a speechless toddler I wanted to know the what, when, and where before it actually happened. When will he talk? When will he look me in the eye? As he continues to make progress and reach milestones like speaking and gesturing, I wanted to know even more. Would he make friends? Would he always need to live with us? Like many parents of an autistic child, I longed for a crystal ball.

When Jack was just three I wanted to see what he would look like as a five-year-old. Now that he's eight I'm anxious to know what the teenage years will bring. Like in Bikram, I spend so much time anticipating the future that I sometimes miss the gift of the present, of Jack standing right in front of me. And so there are days and minutes where I have to resolve to be and to let him be. To stop anticipating.

I've had a lot of success with Bikram yoga overall; my flexibility has greatly improved, and I can even get into postures I originally thought were outrageous. (Specifically, something kind of scary called Camel). But I think my biggest yoga-related accomplishment happened outside of the hot room, in my very own kitchen on a dreary winter afternoon.

Jack and I were working on homework together. After a lot of whining and fussing on his part (and threatening and cajoling on mine), he finally turned off his music and came over to sit at the table with me. When he finished his spelling we moved onto his least favorite subject, math. The minute he saw the fraction-filled sheet he went haywire, running in circles around the kitchen and shrieking about how he couldn't do it, how the numbers were *wrong*, how he didn't understand. I felt my temperature rising. He *could* do it if he would just calm down. How would he ever move onto things like multiplication and division if he couldn't master this simple work? I felt like ripping the sheet into shreds, tossing it into the air like confetti at a parade, and walking away from this hysterical boy.

For fifteen minutes we waged a war over math until at last I took a few deep breaths and found my state of reflection. Inhaling and exhaling deeply, I imagined myself in the yoga studio. I collected my emotions and saw homework hour for what it really was—a time when both Jack and I needed to stretch ourselves, to extend beyond our own limitations and become flexible.

I gave us both a short break. After five minutes I called him back to the table and asked him to look me in the eye so I could explain how to finish the homework. Slightly calmer, Jack looked at me and said, "It's too much! Too many! I can't do them all!" I took a moment to scan the piece of paper, and I realized it wasn't the homework itself that was scaring him but the cluttered grouping of problems and lines. I suggested we use a blank sheet to cover up parts of the homework as we went along, and he happily agreed. Using the back of his spelling paper as white space, he worked steadily down the row of fractions until he was done and then quietly said, "I did it."

I wanted to say, "And so did I."

Because with life, with yoga, and especially with Jack, all I need to do is believe, breathe, and stay in the room.

The Autism in All of Us ❧

LAST WINTER I SIGNED ALL THREE boys up for weekly ski lessons. I downloaded the forms from the website, noting that both the registration and fees needed to be sent within two weeks. Yet for the next week and a half, every time I sat down to fill out the cluttered, busy sheets of paper, I ended up pushing them away with a sigh of disgust. As the deadline loomed closer I kept shuttling the papers from one side of my neatly organized desk to the other.

Just looking at them filled me with dread. And then it occurred to me: like Jack, I hate visual clutter. My eyes glaze right over when I'm faced with confusing forms and busy paperwork.

Disorganization in my own house makes me anxious; I keep our home as free from clutter as possible, and friends and family sometimes make fun of the sparse kitchen and bare countertops. I feel disoriented when I walk into a room brimming with crowded shelves overflowing with knick-knacks, or end tables strewn with newspapers. It's as if my mind can't organize itself and figure out where to focus. Although it takes a fair amount of work to maintain an orderly home with five young kids, I've managed by creating spaces like lockers and toy bins that minimize the perpetual mess of Wii controllers, stray socks, library books, and Legos.

It made me think about what other symptoms of autism spectrum disorder I might have.

A very social person, my issues seem to be more sensory-related. As a kid, the sensation of a rumpled undershirt beneath my clothes made me crazy, and several times a day I ran to the school bathroom to smooth everything out. I cannot stand clothes that are too tight or constricting, and I need to wear soft fabrics. As many of my friends know, much of my sensory issues are wrapped up — literally — in my underwear; for as long as I can remember I've worn them at least two sizes too big. I'm very, very particular about how they fit and, much to Joe's dismay, I've been wearing the same brand since before we got married. (You buy this particular brand in a five-pack from Walmart. They're shiny.) And I firmly believe that people who wear thongs have serious mental problems, which I now realize could mean that my theory of mind may be compromised, too.

Certain noises make me crazy as well. The sound of my children gulping their milk or Joe chewing gum annoys me, and I get pretty overwhelmed in noisy crowds. Jack isn't the only one who doesn't like loud, dog-filled parades or fireworks.

Once I had finished my own self-evaluation, I took a long, cold look at the rest of my family and decided that they, too, could easily reside somewhere along the spectrum. After all, autism is rarely confined to one child within a family; there's usually some spillover. In fact, some research suggests that siblings of an autistic child are more likely to have heightened difficulties with social interactions and communication.

My oldest, Joey, has a hard time paying attention. For a while in school he used a special seat called a wiggle cushion, an inflatable disk that children can sit on and which allows them to move about a bit without feeling like they have to get up from their chair. Joey used it to control his tendency to bounce up and down while sitting. His first-grade teacher even suggested we evaluate him for Attention Deficit Disorder (ADD), another curious stop on the spectrum. At this point he remains diagnosis-free and, having just finished the third grade, seems to be improving his ability to stay focused. In school now he sits without the wiggle-cushion, even if he's not quite wiggle-free.

When she was three, Rose was speech-delayed and received services to help develop her expressive language and articulation. Now, at nearly five years old, her raspy voice echoes non-stop throughout the house (although we're still working on her pronunciation).

Charlie struggles with fairly intense anxiety that often manifests as nightmares or irrational fears. Our niece calls him an "old soul," because, like a little old man, he worries about everything from thunderstorms to whether or not our car is safe enough. He has a tendency to fixate on things like our family's schedule, and he always has a watchful eye out for all of his siblings, especially when we're in public. It's as if he senses some danger the rest of us can't. When we announced we were taking that Disney cruise, Charlie's first response was "Someone will go over the side of the boat!"

Our youngest, Henry, a plump and determined three-year-old, concerns us the most. Out of all of our kids, he's the one whose behavior most resembles Jack's at that age. Although very verbal and social, he's also extremely rigid and inflexible. If I mistakenly place his spoon in his morning cereal instead of letting him put it in the bowl himself, ten minutes of my life can be lost to a volcanic tantrum. He's easily frustrated and has difficulty accepting change. Henry now attends the same integrated preschool Jack used to attend so that we can work on helping him become more flexible, but still his days are punctuated by outburst after outburst, and sometimes it seems like anything can set him off, from someone opening the door before he does, to getting the wrong cup at lunchtime.

Even my husband Joe has his issues, and he's always said that Jack is really just a more exaggerated version of himself. Socially, Joe prefers small groups to large parties, and new situations give him anxiety. Like Jack, he has a tendency to become singularly focused on one topic or project.

All in all, we're a quirky group. I guess the question is this: where does quirky end and autism begin?

I can't count the number of times I've described Jack's autism to friends or family, only to have them say things like "Well, my son doesn't like the sound of fireworks either!" or "I have a hard time sitting still and I'm in my forties!" People have explained how their child has to wear a particular pair of pants every day, or doesn't sleep well at night because of bad dreams, or can't manage a spoonful of soup because of the texture.

Is the whole world autistic?

It's not likely. For one thing, beautiful, quirky, autistic Jack doesn't just struggle with speech or sensory issues or visual clutter or anxiety: he struggles with all of these things, and more. While each of my children shows signs of a specific spectrum characteristic, in Jack those same signs all roll up into one blue-eyed, brown-haired boy.

I decided there's something else standing between the rest of us and a diagnosis: tolerance. Unlike Jack, I've learned to tolerate busy paperwork, rumpled shirts, and the sound of people chewing (barely). Joe has overcome his fear of certain social situations and now even enjoys things like parties and public speaking. We've accomplished this without a lot of therapy or Individual Education Plans. As we traveled through life, my husband and I acquired the necessary coping skills that allow us to stretch ourselves in areas that we normally find uncomfortable. I expect that Jack's brothers and sister will do the same.

Joey, Charlie, Rose, and Henry are not diagnosed with autism, but they do have challenges that we need to understand and solve. And one of the many bright sides to having Jack is this: we've seen a lot of it before. As parents, mine and Joe's job is to give four boys and one girl the skills they need to cope with the challenges they face, whether it be anxiety or sensory processing or the wiggles.

I have not, however, acquired the coping skills to put on a thong. And I probably never will.

Signs ❧

"DO YOU HAVE A *HUSBAND?*" Jack barked at the woman cutting his hair. She looked uncomfortable, quietly murmuring that, no, she was no longer married. "Where did your husband GO?" By the time I had set down my magazine and made my way over to him, Jack was asking her, "Well, if he's GONE then what kind of car does he drive? How many people does it fit?"

It was the first time Jack had met her, and he was performing his usual reconnaissance, a line of questioning that typically begins with marital status and usually circles around to cars and birthdays and favorite songs. If left unchecked, he'll eventually ask the person when they think they're going to die.

Sitting in the overheated barber shop I wished for the millionth time that someone had come up with a universal sign for autism, some sort of hand signal or gesture to let people know that Jack can't read social cues or facial expressions, that the unseen barriers in his brain prevent him from understanding when he's making someone uncomfortable.

It's pretty easy to spot a blind person or a person in a wheelchair. But Jack's disability is buried deep inside his mind; instead of struggling to walk or see or hear, he struggles to communicate, to connect. He struggles with concepts like *empathy* and *cognitive flexibility*. Sometimes it seems like no matter how much we work with him to consider other people's feelings before he opens his mouth and lets the questions fly, he'll still wander up and ask a stranger if their mother is dead yet.

In a perfect world I would make a sign, and everyone around us would nod their head and smile in agreement. *Ah! Autism. Yes, now we understand. We understand why he gets up to stim at a restaurant, galloping between the tables with his fingers in his mouth. We understand why he claps his hands over his ears at the movies.*

I can mostly get away with quietly mouthing the word autism above his head while I run my fingers through his soft, brown hair. That's what I did last time we ate at a Mexican restaurant, when Jack approached a large man and brayed, "Why ARE you so BIG? Did you just EAT too much?"

A universal sign would be so much simpler.

It would really come in handy for those times when the

fine line between *sees the world differently* and *bad behavior* becomes blurred; when people are taken aback by his candor and honesty. It would be helpful at family gatherings, when Jack shouts out things like "What the HELL! That chair is so STUPID!" after he stubs his toe. We could remind our loved ones how hard he's working to express himself, how frustrated he gets when he's anxious or hurt. We could remind them not to judge our blue-eyed boy for the words he chooses, asking that they honor his feelings instead.

I brought up the idea to nine-year-old Joey, and he said, "That would be awesome! I could use it when kids at school say he's weird or when the bus driver gets mad because Jack doesn't always stay in his seat. But what would the sign be?" I admitted that I didn't know.

With such a sign I could dismantle the outer layer Jack's built to protect himself from our confusing world, his bossy and controlling behavior. People could see the sweet, funny, vulnerable boy underneath. The boy who loves bowling and Katy Perry, who wants nothing more in the world than to be with his three brothers and one sister.

It would also come in handy when Jack uses his middle finger to point at things, a habit of his we just can't seem to change.

Joe and I could use it to signal each other in moments when we're both stretched thin by Jack's demands, his needs, his obsessions. When we're both faltering under the emotional weight of an autistic child who talks endlessly about license plates. It would prompt us both to remember that Jack is more than the tantrums, more than the obsessive behavior, more than *I can't do math* and *oh no I am not taking a shower*.

We'd remember that he's the boy who makes us smile every time he walks into the room.

Finally I thought of the perfect sign. Take your hand and hold it up with the fingers extended. Then use your pointer finger and thumb to form a circle: it's the commonly used gesture for *okay*. Because autism really is *okay*.

A Letter *from* Joey ❧

A FEW MONTHS AGO, NINE-YEAR-OLD Joey asked why I was always taking my laptop to the library. "What are you working on?" he asked. He's known about the essays I've written about Jack over the years, and so now I explained how I'm compiling them into a book about autism and our family. A reader himself, Joey's read my articles before and is always interested in any new material I'm developing.

Later that day he wandered back into the kitchen where I was pouring bowls of soup for lunch and said, "You know, I have things to say about being in Jack's family. Maybe I could write a chapter." I was thrilled at his suggestion and agreed that, yes, a chapter from him would really add to the book.

And so one evening, after we'd put all the kids to bed and were lounging on the couch channel-surfing, Joey came back downstairs wearing his deep blue robe and a serious expression.

"Mom. I think I'm ready to start my chapter now."

I opened up a new document in Microsoft Word and told him to write whatever was on his mind.

Once I read it through, I reconsidered whether or not to add it to the book, mostly because I was afraid people wouldn't believe that my nine-year-old son had written this on his own, that many would think that I coached or prompted him to type these words. I assure you, the only editing tips I provided were suggestions for paragraph breaks and a couple of punctuation marks, just to make reading it easier. Otherwise, these words belong solely to Joey.

Autistic Brothering
by Joey Cariello

As Jack's bigger brother, I have a lot of responsibilities. One of my natural responsibilities is to try and keep him calm. My parents don't ask me to do this, I do it because I'm his brother.

But it's not like he needs any help with video games. And, to my surprise, he seems excellent at them. Take the game he plays Fast Draw Showdown, as an example. The idea is to shoot the other person before they shoot you when the bottom of the screen says "draw." He plays other games occasionally. It feels like I have a successor (I'm a video game geek big time). Also he loves the Wii. Though he never plays the computer, Jack is fond of video games.

Sometimes I feel embarrassed if a fourth grader asks about Jack and if he has autism.

Sometimes I think about what life would be if Jack didn't have autism. I think it would be a little bit strange because our family would seem to be perfect.

Life can be hard for Jack. That's why I don't respect anybody who doesn't respect my brothers or my sister. I sometimes get the feeling that I leave Jack out a lot, and I'm being a bad brother. I feel like I spend too much time with my other siblings, so I try to spend more time with him and play the things he likes.

I try to be the best brother I can. (I like him just the way he is even though he has autism.)

The End

Where We Are Now ❧

JACK IS UNAWARE HE HAS AUTISM. Over the summer he asked why he has an aide in school but "not everyone else." I paused for a moment, and then I explained how sometimes he has trouble with things and his aide helps him. When my answer was met with stony silence, I pressed on.

"How does that make you feel, Jack?"

"Fine. Good."

We haven't really considered when and how we'll explain it to him. I figure we'll know when he's ready, although I'm not sure exactly what signs to look for yet. Part of me is looking forward to the time when we can tell him; I think it will be a great relief to discuss his issues openly and to learn his side of the spectrum story.

Out of all of our kids, only Joey and Charlie understand that Jack has a diagnosis. Upon discovering this fact about their brother, each boy asked a version of the same question: "Will he always have autism?"

It's remarkable to me how their first question about Jack's autism echoed the very one I asked the doctor back in 2006 when Jack was first diagnosed. Will he always have it?

From there I quickly moved on to looking for ways to fix him, to repair his deficiencies, to make him normal. But in the past six years I've learned there is no "fixing" when it comes to Jack and his autism. Rather, we need to fix ourselves so that we can better understand and appreciate him.

And so I answered both Joey and Charlie that, yes, Jack will always have autism. When Joey asked if Jack would ever marry, I told him honestly that we had no way of knowing Jack's future, that we're just going to do the best we could to help Jack lead a full, happy life.

Neither boy seemed particularly affected by the knowledge; I think they must have understood all along that something was off, and they don't treat him any differently now that they can put a name to Jack's behaviors. They still argue with him, become frustrated by him, and love him in all the same ways they did before. Occasionally I'll overhear Joey explaining to someone we've just met that "My brother doesn't understand you. He has autism," and when I do my heart simultaneously pulls in two directions: happiness and sorrow.

Jack continues to help me see the world differently, more expansively. While he's still preoccupied with cars, he's moved away from shampoo. His new interests include dates, license plates, countries, and languages. And for the first time his preoccupations don't seem discrete and random; instead, he's relating topics to each other. The other day he asked me, "How do you say 'Honda' in German? 'Bonda?' What? Why are you laughing?"

On any given day you can hear him shout out "California! I see California!" when he spots a particular license plate, or, "Look. Georgia! It's on a Silverado!" Always working to flex his theory of mind, we talk about why people from other states would visit New Hampshire. Together, our whole family creates stories about cars and their license plates. Maybe the man driving the Chevy from Georgia came to visit his dear Aunt Mabel, who is in the hospital because she had an allergic reaction to strawberries. Maybe the family from Florida is house-hunting and planning to move out of the Sunshine State because they want to learn to ski.

He's not usually open to trying new foods, but after checking the atlas to locate Vietnam, he heartily agreed to eat lunch at a Vietnamese restaurant. Over a meal of bok choy and pho, we talked to our server about her country and language. At one point he cried out, "I like this food! It's delicious." Then he asked her how many radios she had in Vietnam.

Of course, it isn't all rainbows and butterflies and pho.

He's still struggling to keep his body regulated, and he has a hard time coping when something is off. On Valentine's Day this year, the whole family was looking forward to a fun meal out at our favorite restaurant—until Jack needed to have a bowel movement and went ballistic. He screamed and cried, running naked from bathroom to bathroom. It wasn't pretty. As I cleaned the walls and toilets (trying not to scream and cry) I explained to the kids that we were going to have to stay in for dinner after all. I think they took it better than I did.

He's still at times quite bossy and controlling. For months he was adamant that we only listen to one certain radio station in the car. This particular station seemed to have a repertoire of exactly six songs from pop artists without a whole lot of talent. It drove me nuts. The second we got in the car he demanded that I "Turn it! Turn to my station! I need to hear it."

Even his latest preoccupation with license plates isn't without peril. After we pull into a parking lot I have to leap out of the car and intercept him because his need to examine every license plate sometimes conflicts with his need to stay away from moving vehicles. He's so single-minded in his pursuit of license-plate knowledge that he abandons safety altogether. At times it feels like I'm chasing a toddler again.

I continue to notice people's kindness relative to Jack. Last spring we hosted Joey's entire class for his ninth birthday. The party's theme was along the lines of "old-fashioned-party-games-with-the-Wii-thrown-in," and we wound up with a group of about twenty-five third graders. Jack was peeved within ten minutes, complaining that "This was so fun until all these kids showed up!"

The party ended with a piñata. It took about five tries for

someone to pull the string hard enough for all of the candy to tumble out, and chaos ensued as all the kids scrambled for loot. They retreated back to the patio to enjoy the treats, and I heard Jack scream, "I wanted a lollipop! I didn't get a lollipop. Lolli-pop!" As I started to make my way over to him, one of Joey's classmates, Aarsh, started to rummage through his own candy bag. A striking Indian boy with a slender frame, Aarsh quickly unearthed the coveted Tootsie Roll pop.

"Jack! Jack! Here's one for you! Take mine."

Standing before both boys in our backyard on an unseasonably warm afternoon in March, I had to look away as my eyes welled with tears. Was Aarsh kinder to Jack because he has autism? I can't say. But he was kind, and because of Jack I noticed it more.

He has started to sing. I often hear him humming and murmuring the words to popular songs as he sits in the backseat and his sweet voice always takes me by surprise. I told him one day that his singing makes my heart smile, and he said, "Hearts. Do not have faces." I agreed and smiled widely with my mouth to show him I was happy. I was rewarded with a quick flash of his gap-filled grin.

His facility with language and nuance also continues to grow. He's always been unintentionally funny, but in the past year we've watched as his sense of humor has blossomed. I asked what we should have for dinner one night, and he chortled, "Snails and snakes!" Then quickly he reminded me, "It was a joke. I was making a joke, I don't like snakes."

Overall he seems to be developing a larger range of

emotions: shame, joy, guilt, empathy. Recently he pinched Rose's arm in the door and quickly rushed to apologize. "I'm sorry. I'm so sorry. I'm apologizing! For an accident!" And his tone of voice is also changing; he's starting to modulate more and lose his robotic quality. I actually miss his monotone a little.

Joe and I talk all the time about whether we'd want Jack to have been born differently, born "normal." Selfishly, I would never want to change a thing about this dazzling boy. Rarely a day goes by when he doesn't delight me in some small way, when Joe and I don't exchange a loving glance over Jack's head about something he's said or done. Without autism, Jack would likely never take note of things like cars, license plates, and radios. And neither would we.

Not long ago Jack asked me what I was working on. I told him I was writing a book and then mentally scrambled to prepare an answer in case he asked what the book was about. But he seemed uninterested and wandered off. About six hours later, over dinner at Bertucci's, he asked out of nowhere, "Will you dedicate this book to us, your family?" And of course I said yes.

Yes, Jack, I will.

Obviously life would be easier for Jack if he didn't have autism. Without autism, Jack could hear the teacher's voice over the faraway sound of a garbage truck driving down the road. He could find the right words to communicate every thought in that brown-haired head of his without a hiccup, and he could tell us just why he's so scared of dogs. He could stop worrying about the wind-chill factor and start eating slimy yogurt. He could always look me in the eye.

In other words, he could be someone else. And I don't want that; I only want my Jack exactly as he is.

I don't wonder so much if he was born wrong, as much as I worry he was born into the wrong family. We are a loud, boisterous bunch, given to sarcastic jokes and teasing. It can't be easy for such a literal child to figure out our sense of humor or to follow a conversation that bounces from person to person so quickly.

But then I sit back and watch.

I watch Jack argue with Joey about the best way to lay out the train tracks. I watch Charlie—always the teacher—explain how our neighbor's dog is on a leash and can't reach him, how he's safe. I watch Jack and Rose page through a book about homemade cupcakes, pointing out their favorites to each other. I watch Jack soothe Henry when he falls in the driveway, telling him "You. Will be Okay. Okay." and then calling for me to help. I marvel at the skills he's gaining, how he engages and expresses himself.

And I watch him respond to each of his siblings differently, growing and learning from every child, and think, not wrong. Just right.

Back when I was pregnant with our fourth child, Jack's preschool teacher remarked to me that the best thing we could do for him was give him siblings. We've heard many stories of couples who limited their number of children because a child had been diagnosed, and I can't say I blame them one bit. I understand fully the amount of work, dedication, and patience raising a child with autism requires, and factoring in the needs of other small children isn't always easy.

But the teacher's comment has remained with me through the years, and I know we did the right thing by providing Jack with three brothers and a sister. He has grown because they push him, and he has learned because they teach him.

Jack fits into our family; it's not the other way around. He always goes to bed when the rest of the kids do, eats what we all eat, and participates in our family's activities. Like the others, he's expected to set the table when it's his turn and to pour himself a bowl of cereal in the morning. We simply don't have the time to revolve our lives around him. With four other kids around, he has his own social circle in which to experiment and play, often bouncing from one child to another throughout the day based on his preference for activity and temperament.

Our family is very, very important to Jack. He prefers to do things "with our whole family," and whenever we suggest a new activity, like miniature golf or bowling, his first question usually is "Can our whole family go?" Recently I bought six stools for our patio because that was how many the area could comfortably fit. Jack was so agitated, so irritated, that we couldn't all sit there that eventually I went back to the store for a seventh stool. He'd rather be squashed all together than apart.

"We need. To all sit together for dinner."

I do have to admit that we're more likely to give in to Jack for some things, like when he asks to eat at a particular restaurant or to read another chapter in our book before bed. Maybe our kids will look back someday and consider Jack the favored child, but I hope instead that they'll see our occasional indulgences as a way to stretch ourselves for him. After all, he stretches himself for us every day.

Years ago, before Joe and I had kids or were even married, I heard a woman explain how her handicapped son was truly a blessing, how she couldn't imagine life with him any other way. And I thought to myself, "A blessing? Pushing Jimmy around in a wheelchair for the rest of your life makes you feel lucky?" But now I get it.

Knowing Jack, we are privy to the development of an exceptional mind. I can't help but feel as though I'm part of something extraordinary when he reminds us that his cousin's birthday is April 1st or that Christmas of 2009 fell on a Friday. Not only because he's capable of amassing such information, but also because he's capable of learning things that don't come naturally to him, like making a joke or telling me that my face looks angry. Or touching a dog.

These seemingly small breakthroughs are colossal leaps for him and they are worth every moment of frustration, every disrupted mealtime, every argument over the radio station.

Sometimes I think I'd like to switch places, just briefly, and see the world through Jack's eyes. What must it be like to see each day as a color? Or to remember the exact day of the week you ate a hot dog in November 2010? I want to experience his discomfort with a hangnail or a loose tooth, just to better understand him, to feel what he feels. I imagine the world of autism to be a magical, confusing, beautiful, frustrating place.

Lately Jack's been talking about going to college, driving a car, having a family. These desires are a big step forward for him, but he expresses them with one foot still firmly planted in his childhood. He wants to "buy the house and live next door" and "drive a Toyota Sequoia like Daddy's so we can all fit in it." He wants to go to a college where he can still come home at night to sleep.

He talks quite a bit about getting married and having kids. "You won't know my kids' names until they are here," he warned me. "Because I don't know them yet, either." I told him I thought that was a good plan.

About four years ago someone coarsely commented that "You don't know how Jack is going to turn out. You don't know if he'll wind up bagging groceries or if he'll live with you for the rest of his life." My heart seized in panic, and the next time we went to the grocery store I shooed him away from the end of the shopping cart, where he usually stands to help load the bags. However, over the years I've grown accustomed to the idea that Jack may live with us for a very long time. Now I welcome it.

But clearly he longs to lead a normal life like everyone else, and I feel as determined as ever to prepare him to do so, to help him reach his full potential. Some days I feel panicked that in the end maybe he won't live the life he's planning for himself and that I will have failed him. In moments when my energy is flagging, when I don't feel like arguing about the radio station or making him put his bowl in the dishwasher, just hearing Jack's hopes and wishes helps me recommit myself.

The irony is that, in my quest to help him reach his full potential, I'm actually reaching my own. I am a far better mother because of him, and he has taught me so much.

Every now and again when I'm driving alone I'll glimpse a license plate from another state, and I feel a small thrill run through me. I catch myself dreaming up reasons why the woman in the car from South Dakota and wearing such large sunglasses would be driving in New Hampshire. I've learned to notice things I might not otherwise see.

I am much stronger than I think. Sometimes that strength means cleaning the bathroom on Valentine's Day, and sometimes it means taking a yoga class to recharge myself. I've also learned never to doubt my gut instinct. From the time he was an infant I knew Jack was different, and if I can be proud of one single thing in my entire life, I'm proud that we never gave up in our quest to help him. Autism is something to embrace, not conquer.

I know, too, that most people are very, very kind to small boys with autism. That's true even when the small boy asks unsavory questions about someone's age or makes them feel uncomfortable about the car they drive.

Jack knows that there are more Hondas in New Hampshire than any other car, and I know that there's more than one road home.

I've learned that, according to Jack, God's last name is "Lord" and that even my literal boy with autism will find his own way with religion and faith, and see it through his own lens.

Sometimes I just have to step back and let the magic unfold on its own, to give Jack a chance to experience the world without my interpretation. I learned this when Jack braved a man and his potcake at a hotel in New Hampshire.

And one of the most interesting lessons I've learned from Jack?

Monday is blue.

A Letter to Jack ✌

Dear Jack,

Happy Birthday! Today you are eight, and I can hardly believe how much you've changed in one year. (Or, as you would say, 365 days.)

Your school year has gone smoothly, and you adapted well to the demands of second grade. You've become an excellent reader, but you struggle to grasp math. In class they asked you to divide two cookies among four kids, and you became visibly agitated. They asked again, and on the third try you blurted, "You need to make more cookies! Two are not enough!"

You were delighted to learn your teacher was pregnant and loved watching her stomach as the baby grew larger. You were even more delighted when she named her new son Jack.

You have a crush on Isabella, a girl in your class, and you asked us to buy the house next door so the two of you can get married and live there when you "turn eighteen and are grown-ups."

Always literal, for a while you insisted on carrots for breakfast and bok choy every night for dinner because we had explained how vegetables keep your body healthy. You still won't touch yogurt or canned peaches, but this year you made a giant leap in communication and explained one night how "slimy foods make my tongue feel weird."

You love marshmallows.

You seem to be happiest around your siblings; the five of you run in a tight pack. Seeing you play and dance with your brothers and sister is perhaps one of my greatest rewards. Hearing you talk, laugh, and even argue with them makes every dirty dish, every wet towel, and every spilled glass of milk worthwhile.

Your latest obsession is the calendar, a big change from last year's preoccupation with cars. You can remember the dates for events small and large, going back as far as three years. As I was preparing dinner one evening, you asked me, "Mom. What color is Monday?" When I answered that I don't see the days of the week like that, you explained how you see days and colors together.

Friday is orange.

Throughout last spring and early summer you wrestled with the slippery grip of anxiety. Within weeks it transformed you from a happy little boy into a child we barely recognized. You were frantic about everything from the wind-chill factor to riding the bus, and simple daily activities like using the bathroom were overwhelming. You barely slept. Terrified, we watched as you started to disappear down a deep, dark hole, and we were powerless to lift you up and out. For two months you never laughed.

Little by little, we found solutions to release anxiety's hold over your mind and spirit, and slowly you returned to your sunny self. I will never take your smile for granted again.

I realized something special this morning as I was writing this letter: for the first time in eight years, I am not panicking on your birthday. I don't have a small pit in my stomach and a tiny voice in my head saying "He's not where he should be, he'll never catch up." At your first birthday I worried you might never speak. When you blew out three candles I was preoccupied with your tantrums, and by the time you turned six I longed for a crystal ball to predict your future.

But today? Today, I'm thrilled to celebrate you, and I think I finally understand that you will always be in exactly the right place, no matter where you are.

This year, Jack, I want to share you with the world. I want people to understand the extraordinary gifts you offer as a result of your autism and the colorful way in which you see life. You have a lot to teach us all.

Love,

Mom

Further Information

Autism is characterized by delays or abnormal functioning before the age of three years in one or more of the following domains: (1) social interaction; (2) communication; and (3) restricted, repetitive, and stereotyped patterns of behavior, interests, and activities.

Autism Spectrum Disorder (ASD) describes a range of conditions classified as pervasive developmental disorders in the Diagnostic and Statistical Manual of Mental Disorders (DSM-IV-TR, 2000). Pervasive developmental disorders include autism, Asperger syndrome, pervasive developmental disorder not otherwise specified (PDD-NOS), childhood disintegrative disorder, and Rett syndrome. These disorders are typically characterized by social deficits, communication difficulties, stereotyped or repetitive behaviors and interests, and in some cases, cognitive delays. Although these diagnoses share some common features, individuals with these disorders are thought to be "on the spectrum" because of differences in severity across these domains.

Early intervention is a system of coordinated services that promotes the child's growth and development and supports families during the critical early years. Early intervention services to eligible children and families are federally mandated through the Individuals with Disabilities Education Act. Starting with a partnership between parents and professionals at this early stage helps the child, family, and community as a whole.

Individualized Education Plan (IEP) refers to a set of individualized objectives for a child who has been labeled with a disability, as defined by federal regulations. In all cases the IEP must be tailored to the individual student's needs as identified by the IEP evaluation process, and must especially help teachers and related service providers (such as paraprofessional educators) understand the student's disability and how the disability affects the learning process.

Joint attention is the shared focus of two individuals on an object. It is achieved when one individual alerts another to an object by means of eye-gazing, pointing or other verbal or nonverbal indications. An individual gazes at another individual, points to an object, and then returns their gaze to the individual.

Pervasive Developmental Disorder (PDD) is considered one of the three autism spectrum disorders (ASD). PDD-NOS is often called *atypical autism.*

Social stories were devised as a tool to help individuals on the autism spectrum better understand the nuances of interpersonal communication so that they could interact in an effective and appropriate manner.

Theory of mind is the ability to attribute mental states such as opinions, beliefs, and knowledge to oneself and others, and to understand that others have opinions, beliefs, and knowledge that are different. Deficits occur in people with autism spectrum disorders, schizophrenia, and attention deficit disorder.

Working memory is the system that actively holds multiple pieces of transitional information in the mind for execution of verbal and nonverbal tasks, such as reasoning and comprehension, and makes them available for further information-processing.

Acknowledgments

I AM GRATEFUL TO THE MANY PEOPLE who inspired, encouraged, and supported me in the effort to write this book.

My heartfelt thank you to Kim Dambach for an off-hand comment in her driveway that jump-started this project, to Audrey Elliott for her suggestions about the title, to Kristin Halverson and Carolyn Cariello for their tireless proofreading and support, to Fiona Bell, Cindy Riker and Mary Johnson for early review and feedback, and to Michael Charney for taking a gamble on *What Color Is Monday?* and for helping me with the tedious editing it takes to produce a book.

I'm grateful to David Minot for giving me a platform in which to start a writing career.

Thank you to Dr. Nancy Sagon for her ongoing wisdom and insight about Jack, autism, and our family.

CARRIE CARIELLO

Also, thank you to Dr. Jan McGonagle for her encouragement and interest in Jack.

I'm thankful to my sisters Sarah Leone, Keri Watterson, Shannon Watterson, Ann Marie Sullivan, Lisa Cariello, and Barbara Cariello for their continued enthusiasm and support, Elaine McSpedon for being my constant touchstone with Jack, to Melissa for providing an outlet every single day and helping to shape my writing through email.

My deep gratitude to Joey, Jack, Charlie, Rose, and Henry for giving me a limitless supply of material and inspiration.

And lastly, to Joe. Thank you for everything. *myitm*

216

About the Author

CARRIE CARIELLO LIVES IN SOUTHERN New Hampshire with her husband, Joe, and their five children. She is a regular contributor to *Autism Spectrum News* and has been published in several local parenting magazines. She has a Master's in Public Administration from Rockefeller College and an MBA from Canisius College in New York.

At best estimate, she and Joe have changed roughly 16,425 diapers.

About the Charity: Autism Speaks

THE GOAL OF AUTISM SPEAKS is to change the future for all who struggle with autism spectrum disorders.

The organization is dedicated to funding global biomedical research into the causes, prevention, treatments and cure for autism; to raising public awareness about autism and its effects on individuals, families and society; and to bringing hope to all who deal with the hardships of this disorder.

Autism Speaks aims to bring the autism community together as one strong voice to urge the government and private sector to listen to our concerns and take action to address this urgent global health crisis.

Autism Speaks. It's time to listen.

Both the author and publisher are proud to donate a portion of the proceeds from the sale of *What Color is Monday?* to this fine organization.

CPSIA information can be obtained at www.ICGtesting.com
Printed in the USA
BVOW03s0207160414

350816BV00002B/32/P

9 780984 792733